MADE FOR A MIRACLE

Made for a Miracle
From Your Ordinary to God's *Extraordinary*

Book
978-1-5018-4138-5
978-1-5018-4139-2 eBook
978-1-5018-4140-8 Large Print

DVD
978-1-5018-4143-9

Leader Guide
978-1-5018-4141-5
978-1-5018-4142-1 eBook

Youth Study Book
978-1-5018-4150-7
978-1-5018-4151-4 eBook

Also by Mike Slaughter

Change the World
Christmas Is Not Your Birthday
Dare to Dream
Down to Earth
Hijacked
Momentum for Life
Money Matters
Real Followers
Renegade Gospel
shiny gods
Spiritual Entrepreneurs
The Christian Wallet
The Passionate Church
UnLearning Church
Upside Living in a Downside Economy

For more information, visit www.MikeSlaughter.com.

MIKE SLAUGHTER

MADE FOR A MIRACLE

From Your Ordinary
to God's *Extraordinary*

Abingdon Press / Nashville

MADE FOR A MIRACLE
FROM YOUR ORDINARY TO GOD'S EXTRAORDINARY

This book is printed on elemental chlorine-free paper.

Library of Congress Cataloging-in-Publication Data has been requested.

ISBN 978-1-5018-4138-5

17 18 19 20 21 22 23 24 25 26 — 10 9 8 7 6 5 4 3 2 1
MANUFACTURED IN THE UNITED STATES OF AMERICA

To Carolyn:
Jesus and you are the two best things
that ever happened to me.

CONTENTS

INTRODUCTION

The life of mortals is like grass,
*   they flourish like a flower of the field;*
the wind blows over it and it is gone,
*   and its place remembers it no more.*
(Psalm 103:15-16)

As I consider my own mortality from the vantage point of my midsixties, I am reminded that it is only what we do for God and people that will live beyond us. After all, we can't take our riches or resumés with us after we die. Only the fruit produced during our brief tenure on this earth—that time represented by the dash between the two dates on our tombstone—will outlast us.

Every human being has this innate desire to leave a legacy. I remember first grasping this deep desire to find meaning for our lives in a psychology class during my undergraduate days at the University of Cincinnati, as we read Viktor E. Frankl's book *Man's*

Search for Meaning (1946). I have witnessed time and time again in my forty-five years as a pastor that the key to helping people connect into the life of the body is through finding life meaning, not attending more church meetings.

This drive for meaning is also at the core of why we love to experience God's miracles. Miracles remind us that there is something more to this life than simply going to work, paying the bills, and playing a little golf on Saturdays. Deep down inside we desire action, adventure, or anything that pulls us out of what sometimes feels like the "rinse and repeat" humdrum of everyday life.

It's also true, however, that many of us expect our miracles to be like magic. We sit back waiting for God as master magician to wave the wand and pull our highly coveted rabbit out of the tall silk hat. Yet God isn't in the magic business, but the miracle business! We have a responsible part to play.

In the chapters ahead, we will explore this possibility for miracles in all of our lives, revealing that each of us was made for a miracle. At the same time, the miracle business is not a passive one. Miracles come at a cost and require something of us. Throughout *Made for a Miracle*, we will explore how Scripture reveals that when God acts, it's always through people.

In fact, God's miracles throughout both the Old and New Testaments reveal that miracles typically have two dimensions: divine intervention *and* human responsibility. That's why the proud army commander Naaman had to wash himself in the humble Jordan River for his leprosy to be cured. It's why five thousand households on a Galilean hillside were fed only after Jesus told his disciples, "*You* give them something to eat." It's why Lazarus was only completely free from the trappings of death after his neighbors helped remove his grave cloths. God is inviting us to be full partners in this miracle-making business.

To experience miracles, you also must realize that miracles aren't *for* you; God releases miracles *through* you for God's purposes in the lives of other people. Where is God calling you to heal, teach, preach, redeem, and restore that which is broken, struggling, or suffering in the world God loves?

Now, if your reaction at this point is that you feel unqualified for being a copartner in God's miracle-making ventures, no worries. It's not our ability but our availability that God is most interested in.

Ready to transform your ordinary into God's extraordinary for bringing about miracles on planet earth? Let's get started.

1
YOU WERE MADE
FOR A MIRACLE

1

YOU WERE MADE FOR A MIRACLE

When Jesus called the Twelve together, he gave them power and authority to drive out all demons and to cure diseases, and he sent them out to proclaim the kingdom of God and to heal the sick.

(Luke 9:1-2)

Can you remember when the call to follow Jesus became personal? A personal God calling comes in many different ways and at different life stages. For many, the calling is progressive, over a period of time or through a series of events. For the young teenager Mary, God's calling came through the messenger Gabriel (Luke 1:26-38). Maybe you are one of those who first began to personalize the call of Jesus through contagious messengers of God in your teen years. Jesus' call in my own life occurred sometime between age seventeen and eighteen.

God's calling came to Joseph in a dream (Matthew 1:18-24). Our dreams are sometimes referred to as the "thin space" between the spiritual and physical. Haven't you ever had an important idea or answer to a question you've been pondering for a while that comes to you in the middle of the night? The nocturnal revelation is so important that you get out of bed and write it down so you won't forget the inspired thought by morning.

Saul, who would later become the apostle Paul, found his calling in the disruptive form of a blinding light. A disruptive crisis event will often awaken the longing for spiritual guidance and intervention. Because of crisis, church basements and fellowship halls become spaces for Twelve-Step groups and divorce recovery groups, as well as for financial planning groups that help people overcome the overwhelming burden of debt. Many of these folk would never have darkened the doors of a church building without experiencing a crisis and the overwhelming need for a power greater than themselves.

People in crisis not only feel a need for a greater power; they seek it in the company of others. Note that in our scripture, Jesus called the original Twelve "together." As we journey together in supportive community, we find in Jesus the power and authority to drive out our personal demons and to heal our diseases.

LIFE-ALTERING QUESTIONS

When the call of Jesus becomes personal, God is no longer just a nominal religious tradition or philosophical idea. This life-defining moment marks the GPS course for the rest of your life. By no means do you have all the answers, but you do begin to ask life-altering questions. Saul asked, "Who are you, Lord?" when he was blinded on the road to Damascus (Acts 9:5). Saul wasn't the first to have asked this question or the first person who was uncertain about Jesus' identity. In Luke 9:7-9, after hearing news about Jesus' ministry, Herod is described as "perplexed because some were saying that John had been raised from the dead, others that Elijah had appeared, and still others that one of the prophets of long ago had come back to life." Herod then said, in essence, "I beheaded John the Baptist myself. This can't be him. Who is this guy?"

My own conversion happened through a perfect storm—failing grades in high school, members of the band I was playing in arrested for illegal drug possession, and the looming possibility of being drafted for the Vietnam War. For the first time, I began to read the Bible that I had been given in third grade. And I am convinced that it was by divine guidance that I started with the four Gospels. Jesus seemed to jump right off of the pages. He was not the meek and mild, white and tamed, watered-down messiah that has been portrayed by many traditionalists in the Western church. Jesus was neither a conservative literalist who believed in an eye for an eye and a tooth for a tooth, nor a liberal progressive who denied the reality of the miraculous through supernatural intervention. I asked, along with Saul, "Who are you, Lord?"

Pontius Pilate, the Roman governor of Judea from AD 26 to 36, was confronted with a life-altering point of decision when Jesus was brought to him by the Jewish authorities: "What shall I do, then, with Jesus who is called the Messiah?" (Matthew 27:22).

These questions, asked by Paul, Herod, and Pilate, are the most important questions we can ask in our lifetime. Don't make Pilate's mistake of trying to remain neutral about Jesus or make Jesus a problem for others to solve. Pilate listened to the voices of the crowd who called for Jesus' crucifixion rather than to the heart voice of his own conscience.

Jesus himself, in Luke 9:20, asked those following him this all-important question: "Who do you say I am?" Only Peter was quick to respond, "God's Messiah." Oftentimes people aren't prepared to respond quite so promptly as Peter did. That's to be expected. For many of us, conversion into a new life in Christ is an over-time process, not an instantaneous or spontaneous reaction.

How have you answered these questions? Or maybe a better way to ask is how are you still answering the question of Jesus' call to follow? The answers can only be discovered in the act of following and not before. Don't wait for definitive answers to these ultimate questions. Commit to being all in, follow Jesus fully, and begin to discover the answers in life's miraculous outcomes!

THE MIRACLE OF TRANSFORMATION

Have you noticed that it was the nonreligious, ordinary, socially unacceptable, and religiously incorrect types whom Jesus chose to lead his movement? His twelve disciples alone are proof enough. Peter was an impulsive laborer in the fishing industry; Simon was a zealot, a first-century version of today's alt-right movement; and Matthew collected taxes for the hated Roman occupiers. I never lose the awe and wonder that Jesus chose someone like me, who finished his junior year in high school with four Fs and a D-, to be a pastor. Or, that Jesus called someone to write books who had never read one! (Well, that may be a slight exaggeration.) Jesus was always calling ordinary women and men who would become, through the Spirit's work of transformation, extraordinary!

At this moment, you may feel no sense of the extraordinary in your life, much less the miraculous. You might be stuck in a job you hate or even be unemployed. Perhaps you are dealing with the pain of loss through divorce, sickness, or the death of a loved one. Take heart! Jesus' last journey to Jerusalem reminds us that true transformation and new life come through pain and even death: "Very truly I tell you, unless a kernel of wheat falls to the ground and dies, it remains only a single seed. But if it dies, it produces many seeds" (John 12:24). The truly miraculous is experienced as we dare to journey with Jesus in the sacrificial way of the cross. "Whoever wants to be my disciple must deny themselves, and take up their cross daily and follow me. For whoever wants to save their life will lose it, but whoever loses their life for me will save it" (Luke 9:23-24). In this process of transformation, we die to self-interest and self-reliance and discover our true identity and life purpose in Christ.

Jesus gave his followers new names to represent their new identities. Simon became Peter, and Saul became Paul. Almost two millennia earlier, the patriarch Jacob had a series of relational and business setbacks that led to emotional, restless nights of sleep. He had been, let's say, less than upright in his relationships and business dealings, even cheating his own family members. However, Jacob's all-night wrestling match with God ultimately transformed his character. God's message came to Jacob when Jacob was willing to accept God's true calling and purpose for his life: "Your name will no longer be Jacob, but Israel, because you have struggled with God and with humans and have overcome" (Genesis 32:28).* From that day forward, Jacob always walked with a slight limp, a reminder of his own daily need and dependence upon God. Jacob found life's gains through his pain.

When you find yourself in a painful period of your life, or in a time when doubt and skepticism far exceed your faith, hang on and refuse to let go of God's amazing grace and ultimate purpose for your life. You are fearfully and wonderfully made. All of us must remember that God "created my inmost being; you knit me together in my mother's womb" (Psalm 139:13). God reminds us,

---

* The name Jacob can mean "holder of the heel" or "supplanter," but it is also frequently translated as "cheat," apropos considering Jacob's successful efforts to cheat his brother Esau out of his inheritance.

as he did the prophet Jeremiah, "For I know the plans I have for you…plans to prosper you and not to harm you, plans to give you hope and a future" (Jeremiah 29:11).

A Pharisee named Nicodemus, who was also a member of the Jewish ruling council, came to Jesus under the cover of darkness, seeking wisdom about Jesus' mission: "Rabbi, we know that you are a teacher who has come from God. For no one could perform the signs you were doing if God were not with him" (John 3:2). In answering Nicodemus, Jesus used the analogy of new birth to describe spiritual awakening: "Very truly I tell you, no one can see the kingdom of God unless they are born again" (John 3:3).

Human suffering and brokenness, caused by sin, resulted in us losing our identity as children of God and forgetting that we are fearfully and wonderfully made. The process of transformation in spiritual awakening allows us to see with new eyes both who we are in Christ and why we are here. Jesus is the fullest revelation of the person and character of God. But Jesus not only revealed God in the flesh, he also revealed what it means to be human. This is why Jesus often referred to himself as "the son of man."

OUR IDENTITY IN CHRIST

You can tell a lot about where people find their identity and what they value by observing their T-shirts and tattoos. One winter evening at the end of the Christmas holidays, my wife, Carolyn, and I treated our daughter's family to dinner at one of our favorite Mexican restaurants in the mountains of north Georgia. My son-in-law, Brendan, is from the Boston area and is ape-wild about the Red Sox. Right in the middle of finishing off the corn chips and salsa, he yelled across the room to a man sitting at a booth three tables away; "Hey, I love that T-shirt you're wearing!" The man got up and walked over to our table…and you may have guessed what happened next. Two avid Red Sox fans found each other in the Georgia mountains and entered into a discussion about the team's stats from the previous season.

When our son, Jonathan, turned twenty-one, he designed a tattoo showing a crown of thorns encircling the ancient Greek letters representing Jesus' name in the center. While visiting my daughter's family in Boston together, he and I visited a downtown tattoo studio and had the design inked on our shoulders, permanently reminding us who we are and why we are here.

We remind ourselves of our true identity when we remember and proclaim our baptism. Matthew tells us in his Gospel that when Jesus was baptized by his cousin John, a voice was heard from heaven saying, "This is my Son, whom I love; with him I am well pleased" (Matthew 3:17). This is who we are! You are God's son. You are God's daughter. And with you God is well pleased. Nothing, absolutely nothing, can ever separate you from that love or status!

Now, if you are anything like me you may be having serious doubts about God's unconditional love. I am well aware of my own failures and shortcomings in living up to Jesus' radical call, "Follow me!" We need to remember, however, that immediately after Jesus' own baptism, the Spirit led him into the wilderness, where he faced incredible temptations. Three times the devil tempted Jesus to doubt his identity in God the Father by changing the absolute "This is my Son, whom I love" to "If you are the Son of God, then..." In other words, the devil said, "You can't be sure. Prove it!" But Jesus didn't have to prove what God the Father had proclaimed, and neither do we.

Don't listen to the voice saying that you're less than the person you are called to be—that you're not worthy, you have limited potential, you're not college material, you'll never be more than average. Don't confuse these whispers of darkness with the promises of God. As Jesus said, you are destined for a life of fruitfulness. You are highly valued. You have been made for greatness.

> *"You did not choose me, but I chose you and appointed you so that you might go and bear fruit—fruit that will last—and so that whatever you ask in my name the Father will give you."*
>
> (John 15:16)

When you hear those tempting voices of darkness that question your identity, just say, "I am baptized—*kiss off!*"

Jacob, like Peter and Paul and countless others through the centuries, found his true identity and source of authority in God the Father. So did Loretta Ross-Gotta, a retired Presbyterian clergywoman who directs the Sanctuary Foundation for Prayer, a retreat center in Topeka, Kansas. She wrote in her work, *Letters from the Holy Ground,*

> When we seek our authority in others, in wealth and possessions, in physical or intellectual prowess, instead of in God the Father, we will be continually defending and protecting this authority and threatening any who might question it. When our authority comes from God, we respect and value our power to bless and to curse. We do not use words carelessly. We make sober, wise judgments and take responsibility for the power to create and beget and parent that which has been entrusted to us.[1]

It is in the daily denial of self-will—saying yes to God's will—that we are empowered to become a healing source of God's miracles in people's lives around us. As Jesus promised,

> *"Very truly I tell, you, whoever believes in me will do the works I have been doing, and they will do even*

greater things than these, because I am going to the
Father. And I will do whatever you ask in my name, so
that the Father may be glorified in the Son."

(John 14:12-13)

Faith and works cannot be separated. Faith is always demonstrated through action. Every miracle has two components that must work in tandem: divine intervention and human initiative. Both components are required for God-initiated, Jesus-multiplying miracles. Remember, when the disciples wanted to dismiss for dinner five thousand hungry families sitting on a hillside listening to Jesus speak, Jesus said, "*You* give them something to eat" (Mark 6:37, emphasis added). He prayed, then used the disciples' hands and feet, along with a few loaves and fishes, to make a miracle in which the divine and the human intersected. We will look at this more closely in a moment.

PARTICIPANTS IN THE MIRACULOUS

In Jesus' humanity we are awakened to our own potential: "The things I do, you will do, and even greater!" What an amazing promise! The same divine, miraculous power that resided in the man Jesus also indwells in each of us through the Holy Spirit. As the apostle Paul put it,

And if the Spirit of him who raised Jesus from the dead
is living in you, he who raised Christ from the dead will
also give life to your mortal bodies because of his Spirit
who lives in you.

(Romans 8:11)

I find it incredibly helpful to remind myself of our God-given potential outlined by Paul:

23

> *I pray that the eyes of your heart may be enlightened*
> *in order that you may know the hope to which he has*
> *called you, the riches of his glorious inheritance in his*
> *people, and his incomparably great power for us who*
> *believe. That power is the same as the mighty strength*
> *he exerted when he raised Christ from the dead....*
>
> (Ephesians 1:18-20)

The same power that raised Christ from the dead is working in and through you and me! Jesus' miraculous works that he performed in his thirty-three years on earth are continued and exponentially multiplied through his followers in every generation. We literally become the presence of Christ acting to meet the needs of the world in the present time.

Jesus' mission becomes our life mission, as read from the Book of Isaiah by Jesus when he announced his messianic mission in his hometown synagogue: "to proclaim good news to the poor...to bind up the brokenhearted...to proclaim freedom for the captives...and release from darkness for the prisoners..." (Isaiah 61:1). Jesus' followers are empowered to "rebuild the ancient ruins...restore the places long devastated...renew ruined cities..." (Isaiah 61:4). The transformed in Christ become Christ's transformers.

Continue to follow the pattern of Jesus' authority as it was first given to twelve of his disciples and then to seventy-two more. The Twelve

> *set out and went from village to village, proclaiming the*
> *good news and healing people everywhere.... After this*
> *the Lord appointed seventy-two others and sent them*
> *two by two ahead of him to every town and place where*
> *he was about to go.... The seventy-two returned with*

joy and said, "Lord, even the demons submit to us in
your name."

(Luke 9:6; 10:1, 17)

This is what it means to be the church. We are Jesus' disciples, who have been called together, given power and authority to drive out evil, heal sickness and addiction, and proclaim God's authority to all people. Each of us brings our unique set of spiritual gifts, talents, and resources to function together as Christ's body and carry out Jesus' mission in the world.

John Henry Newman (1801-1890) was a priest, poet, and theologian who is perhaps best known for the Newman Centers named in his honor at colleges and universities across the United States. In his sermon "God's Will the End of Life," Newman stated:

> Everyone who breathes, high and low, educated and ignorant, young and old, man and woman, has a mission, has a work. We are not sent into this world for nothing; we are not born at random....God sees every one of us; He creates every soul...for a purpose....As Christ has His work, we too have ours; as He rejoiced to do His work, we must rejoice in ours also."[2]

EXPONENTIAL INCREASE

We must release the gifts that God has entrusted to our care in order to experience a lifetime of miraculous increase. This is a fundamental life principle that has proven to be true in my experience. We find life in the act of giving our life gifts to others.

After Jesus' twelve disciples returned and gave an accounting of their mission, he retreated with them to a beautiful, semi-mountainous area along the northern shores of the Sea of Galilee. Stories of Jesus' miraculous healings had spread quickly through the surrounding Galilean towns and villages. But fame comes with a price that sunglasses and baseball caps can't hide. The pressing crowds became overbearing, and at times escape seemed impossible.

Anyone who has been around long enough might remember the unexpected crowd of over four hundred thousand people who flocked to the Woodstock Festival, held on a dairy farm in New York State in August of 1969. Food vendors, among others, were completely unprepared. Similarly, you can just imagine how Jesus' disciples reacted: "Send the crowd away so they can go to the surrounding villages and countryside and find food and lodging, because we are in a remote place here" (Luke 9:12).

Now, I want you to catch what Jesus said next. In a shocking reversal of expectation, he shifted responsibility back to the disciples: "You give them something to eat" (v. 13). Remember, God is in the miracle business, and miracles have two components: divine intervention + human initiative = miraculous.

Not surprisingly, the disciples responded with disbelief: "We only have five loaves of bread and two fish" (v. 13)— a quantity of food that was totally inadequate to feed a crowd that included five thousand heads of households, perhaps as many as twenty thousand people.

All of us have been there or will be at some point in our lives. You may be a single parent working two jobs, just trying to pay the next insurance bill. You may be a pastor in a dying church with resistant church members who don't seem to give a damn about the kingdom of God. Your doctor's office has just called with discouraging test results. The principal of your local high school has informed you that your child has a drug problem. Your debt load has become unbearable, and you've just found out that your Fortune 500 employer is about to close more than 150 of its outlets and lay off two thousand people.

Where do you find the emotional and physical resources to survive these tumultuous times? You're asking the wrong question. God's plan for your life is to take you beyond surviving to thriving. Remember God's promise:

> The LORD will make you the head, not the tail. If you
> pay attention to the commands of the LORD your God
> that I give you this day and carefully follow them, you
> will always be at the top, never at the bottom.
> *(Deuteronomy 28:13)* *

Notice the conditional nature of the passage. *If* you pay attention to the commands and *carefully follow them*, then you will experience the abundant life that Jesus promises. So, what did the Lord Jesus command that day on the hillside? "You give them something to eat."

Follow along with me now in Luke's account of Jesus' miracle of multiplication. The exponential miracle began to unfold when the disciples became willing to let go and let God. It seemed totally illogical. How could so little do so much for so many? But you and I, together in community, become the source for God's miracles. We find life by giving our gifts of life—both spiritual and physical— for God's provision and saving work in the lives of others. We must release in order to experience God's miracle of increase; we must lose our life to find it.

Jesus blessed the meager meal the disciples had gathered and then entrusted them with the mission of distribution. Disciples of Jesus are called to be God's FedEx delivery system throughout the planet. And, yes, we deliver on weekends and holidays. We need to

---

* A caution here about "always be at the top, never at the bottom." Jesus' version of the top is different from the secular understanding. The way of the cross turns our definitions of success, abundance, and leadership upside down. The leader committed to Jesus' way is one who washes others' feet.

remind ourselves daily that we are God's way of delivering heaven's resources into the lives of God's children: "and he sent them out to proclaim the kingdom of God and to heal the sick" (Luke 9:2).

How are you releasing your life gifts for God's increase of blessing in the lives of others?

A LIFETIME MISSION

"No one who puts a hand to the plow and looks back is fit for service in the kingdom of God."

(Luke 9:62)

After more than thirty-eight years of leading Ginghamsburg Church, I turned over the leadership on June 28, 2017, to my friend Chris Heckaman. Chris had been a student of our ministry for almost thirty years. He first heard me speak at a men's breakfast when he was a sophomore at Bowling Green State University.

People began to refer to my transition as "Mike Slaughter's retirement." The concept of "retirement" is in no sense a biblical option for one who has put his hand to the plow of Christ's kingdom work. I did not retire from the mission to which I have been called. Jesus' call to follow has moved me forward to God's next: to give my full attention to coaching young pastors, writing and speaking on behalf of the global church, and to be an advocate against injustice in all forms.

As long as we have breath in our bodies, God will always have a next. We have been put on this earth to be God's difference makers. As Jesus reminded his disciples following his resurrection, "As the Father has sent me, so I am sending you" (John 20:21). Young or old, age isn't a factor. "Don't let anyone look down on you because you are young, but set an example for the believers in speech, in conduct, in love, in faith and in purity" (1 Timothy 4:12).

Moses had his transformational burning-bush moment at the age of eighty. He spent the last forty years of his life obediently leading God's people toward the place of promise. Those years were full of promise and yet came with frustrations, setbacks, and internal battles. There had to be many occasions during those wilderness years when Moses wished that God would have called someone else.

There are wilderness seasons in all our lives, times when we are given over to doubts, wondering if the place of promise even exists. Mother Teresa had her own crisis of faith. Her secret letters show that she spent almost fifty years without sensing the presence of God in her life.[3] Mother Teresa, like the patriarch Jacob, refused to let go of the God mission for which she was called.

Moses never reached the place of promise that he was leading God's people to. But God did allow Moses to view the place of promise from Mount Nebo, on the Jordanian side of the northern Dead Sea. Moses was able to see at his death the exponential future return that would be the result of his lifetime investment. Moses never lost sight of his God-given life purpose: "Moses was a hundred and twenty years old when he died, yet his eyes were not weak nor his strength gone" (Deuteronomy 34:7).

For my own life, I have identified five biblical practices for sustaining physical health, personal integrity, and strategic focus to ensure that I maintain momentum for the long haul, as described in my book *Momentum for Life*. I continue to dare to dream God's preferred future for my life. The commitment to maintain daily personal disciplines that allow me to sustain momentum for my life's calling is absolutely essential as I continue to live into God's miracle.

REFLECTION

For those of you who have had a conversion experience, think back to that experience and consider the following:

- How did Jesus speak to you then? How does Jesus speak with you now?

- In a worship message called "Name Change," I asked listeners to pull a sticker name tag out of their worship bulletin and to write on it what their "name" was before encountering Jesus. Later in worship, they were directed to mark out that name and to instead write on the sticker their new name in Christ. One woman later shared with me that her name before Christ was "hopeless." After meeting Jesus, her name changed to "hope-full." Reflect on your "name change" and what it means for Christ's call upon your life today.

- Where are you sensing God at work right now in your church or community through divine intervention intersecting with human initiative? How might you become a part of the miracle?

- Have you been praying for a miracle? What opportunities might you have to add your human initiative or resources toward God's divine intervention in your family, neighborhood, or workplace?

2
MIRACLES COME WITH A COST

2

MIRACLES COME
WITH A COST

He told them: "Take nothing for the journey—no staff,
no bag, no bread, no money, no extra shirt."

(Luke 9:3)

What was Jesus talking about? "Take nothing for the journey"?
This is the complete antithesis to all I know about the need for
self-care and economic responsibility. It's one of those instances
in which Jesus could have used the help of a public relations
specialist.

Just take a look at some of the outrageous statements Jesus made
when he was becoming a public sensation. Luke reports that "large
crowds" were turning out to Jesus' events. Now, you or I might

have done something strategic and given them a welcome bag with a coffee mug silk-screened with the church logo. Not Jesus!

> *"If anyone comes to me and does not hate father and mother, wife and children, brothers and sisters—yes, even their own life—such a person cannot be my disciple. And whoever does not carry their cross and follow me cannot be my disciple."*
>
> *(Luke 14: 26-27)*

Wow! What are you doing, Jesus? You have what every church leader prays for—not an empty seat to be had. Now, just when we expect you to explain what you really meant by the word *hate* (as we contemporary pastors do in trying to fill the role of public relations specialist), you go on to state emphatically, "In the same way, those of you who do not give up everything you have cannot be my disciples" (v. 33). A decision to follow you clearly calls for a radical lifestyle adjustment. All-in, or nothing!

Jesus recognized that the time for the fulfillment of his life mission was at hand. With resolution and purpose, he set out for what would become his final trip to Jerusalem. Ultimately he would be crucified and would rise from the dead. But for Jesus, the miracle of the resurrection would come with a cost, and the same is true for us.

SETTING PRIORITIES

Jesus' personal encounters along the way to the cross have much to teach us about our own life priorities. For example, Jesus often spoke about personal money matters and the responsibility to use these resources for the well-being of the poor and disenfranchised. When he encountered a man of status and means, Jesus reminded the man that a commitment to keep God's moral commandments is incomplete without making deep personal sacrifices for those who lack life's basis necessities. Jesus cut through the man's incomplete understanding of the path to eternal life when he said to the man: "You still lack one thing. Sell everything you have and give to the poor, and you will have treasure in heaven. Then come, follow me" (Luke 18:22).

Dietrich Bonhoeffer paid the ultimate price of discipleship through his death by hanging in the Nazi Flossenbürg Concentration Camp. As Bonhoeffer's biographer Eric Metaxas summarized one of Bonhoeffer's core beliefs, "Being a Christian is less about cautiously avoiding sin than about courageously and actively doing God's will."[1] This gospel mandate challenges my own margins of comfort, which were provided by the accident of longitude and latitude that brought my arrival through birth into American citizenship. I confess that I have to do serious introspection when it comes to the conflicting values of the kingdom of God and the American dream. Our priorities become distorted when we forget our ultimate God calling and make life all about getting a great education so we can have a prosperous career, raise a family, have a house, enjoy two cars with all the toys, take a yearly vacation, retire, and then simply enjoy life.

Jesus made this gospel mandate painfully clear to a man in the crowd who sought him out, consumed with his own temporal financial future: "Teacher, tell my brother to divide the inheritance with me" (Luke 12:13). How often have we been guilty of doing the same, asking God to bless and promote our own self-focused life plans? Jesus was quick to respond: "Watch out! Be on your guard against all kinds of greed; life does not consist in an abundance of possessions" (v. 15).

To further illustrate his point, Jesus went on to tell a parable about a rich fool who accumulated wealth without understanding

MADE FOR A MIRACLE

his responsibility for God's greater kingdom purpose: "But God said to him, 'You fool! This very night your life will be demanded from you. Then who will get what you have prepared for yourself?'" Jesus continued, "This is how it will be with whoever stores up things for themselves but is not rich toward God" (vv. 20-21).

We must not rationalize or spiritualize Jesus' actual, physical demands to follow him by sacrificing our time, life gifts, and financial resources for the least and the lost. We are called by the Master to use our affluence for the purpose of God's influence in the lives of people who have neither. Life is found in the intentional acts of giving our life gifts to others.

LIFESTYLE PRIORITIES

Far too many of us simply believe in Jesus; far too few of us actually follow. There are eighty-seven references in the four Gospels where Jesus says, "Follow me," and only two references where Jesus says, "Believe in me." Can you imagine how different the world would look if Christians followed Jesus and didn't just believe in him?

The great Indian leader Mahatma Gandhi rejected Christianity but not Christ. When Christian missionaries asked him why, Gandhi told them, "I like your Christ; I do not like your Christians. Your Christians are so unlike your Christ."[2] Luke mentions three encounters that Jesus had with potential followers almost immediately after he began his final journey to Jerusalem (see Luke 9:57-62). In each encounter, Jesus spoke about setting priorities: lifestyle priorities, schedule priorities, and relationship priorities.

In the first encounter, Jesus was approached by a potential follower: "As they were walking along the road, a man said to him, 'I will follow you wherever you go.'" Jesus immediately challenged the man to consider the demanding nature of a follower's life: "Foxes have dens and birds have nests, but the Son of Man has no place to lay his head" (Luke 9:57-58). Jesus was in effect asking the man, "Do you really understand what you're signing up for?" In other words, Jesus was talking about lifestyle priorities.

Shortly after I graduated from seminary, Carolyn and I moved to Cincinnati to accept a full-time position in youth ministry. The church was gracious in providing a wonderful townhouse for us to move into, but it would not become available until two months after our arrival. An older gentleman who had recently been widowed was kind enough to allow us to move into his partially finished attic. The room was sparsely furnished, with an antique bed whose ancient springs squeaked with every movement and a weathered picnic table that had obviously been in storage for some time.

We were able to use his kitchen for preparing our meals and would tread down the attic stairs any time we needed to use the bathroom. Cincinnati can be terribly humid in the summer, and of course the attic was the only non-air-conditioned part of the house. On our first Saturday evening before our first Sunday in our new appointment, I lay in the creaky bed next to Carolyn and quoted Jesus' reminder: "Foxes have dens and birds have nests, but the Son of Man has no place to lay his head."

Carolyn and I thanked God for the privilege to be called into such an adventure, even if it would mean a lifetime of inconvenience and discomfort. This is what following Jesus is all about. It really comes down to the lifestyle choices that we are willing to make. We live more simply so that others may simply live!

I need to make a confession. The commitment was much easier to make when I was twenty-seven. Through the years we learn to adapt to different standards of living. Incomes tend to grow with time. How did we ever make it on $5,200 a year? Our children grow up, are educated, and leave home. Many of us have more expendable income to spend on the nonessentials. Now in our midsixties, Carolyn and I tend to focus on bucket list dreams, and our somedays are now.

Regardless of your age, the directive of Jesus remains the same, and God will deploy your gifts for bringing about miracles. Abraham was seventy-five when God called him to leave everything he had ever known, and he "obeyed and went, even though he did not know where he was going" (Hebrews 11:8).

GOD'S CALL IN SOUTH SUDAN

A few of my personal heroes have made extraordinary contributions to the kingdom, risking forward toward God's miracles well into the second half of life. Two of those heroes are Fred and Libby Dearing.

Fred, a retired ordained elder in The United Methodist Church, spent more than three decades in local church ministry and then served an additional seven years as a district superintendent in the Holston Conference of Tennessee. I use the word *retired* loosely. In 2011, at the age of sixty-seven and at the request of the Holston Conference's bishop, Fred relocated with his wife, Libby, to Yei, South Sudan, as a United Methodist "volunteer in mission" to serve in the unpaid position of district superintendent for all of South Sudan. Fred and Libby would spend the next five years of their lives in some of the most exciting, frustrating, and challenging circumstances any two people could conceivably experience.

Fred first fell in love with the people of South Sudan when he traveled there as part of a three-person team in 2006, to assess whether his conference should establish a larger mission in what was five years later to be the newest country on the planet. In long days of meeting with leaders of the South Sudanese church in Yei, Fred heard the frustration and discouragement of this fledgling church and community, as church leaders shared how they felt abandoned by the larger church and disappointed by unfulfilled promises. Several visitors from the United States had shown up promising help, but none had ever returned. Fred said, "I then knew for sure that we would be back. I just didn't realize at that time that the 'we' would mean me."

When he and Libby arrived for their mission in South Sudan, it didn't turn out to be exactly what Fred had expected. There certainly were some rewards! Small churches that had been planted in the region surrounding Yei were hungry to bloom and grow, develop leaders, and reach neighbors for Christ. Fred, Libby, and their team were able to help train these church leaders, start micro-business opportunities, begin agricultural programs, and develop homes and support for South Sudanese orphans—a particular passion of Libby's.

On the other hand, some of the original Yei church leaders turned out to be in the "church business" for their own personal gain. There were even accusations about Fred, but none ever resulted in government action against Fred, since all accusations were unfounded. But it certainly took its toll upon Fred, who chose to remain faithful to his call and his responsibility despite the stress.

Libby's special interest in the orphans led her to start the orphanage she had dreamed of for years. She admitted, "There is nothing in my history, personality, or experience that remotely suggested I could accomplish this huge task. But, that is the way God works. In hindsight I see that he gave me this 'assignment' because it truly pointed to him. Without God's equipping, preparing, and guiding me, I could not have even started such a feat."

Over time, Libby and her team were able to provide care and love for thirty-six orphans. To help the children still feel like a part of a loving family and community, the orphanage was designed in the form of small houses located in close proximity, where one "mama" and six children could live together. Of course, funding was a significant challenge, but Libby described how one US church, which had committed to raise $80,000 for the orphanage, wound up raising $200,000 one Christmas. The God provision continued, and a second, smaller orphanage opened in 2015.

In 2016 the Dearings, along with all other non-African church staff, had to leave South Sudan because of the civil unrest and famine that were rocking the fledgling country. However, the church leaders they had supported found their way to refugee camps in Uganda, and through some amazing God interventions, all the children in the orphanage were also brought safely into Uganda.

Today Fred and Libby, sometimes on site and sometimes from within the United States, continue to serve and support the good work that God had started in these lives. Although the Dearings pray for peace and stability in South Sudan, Fred admits that in some ways the move to Uganda has opened up new doors of provision, training, and education for the relocated South Sudanese. Fred is working with six South Sudanese pastors in training. These leaders will be ordained within two years, one of whom will replace Fred, now age seventy-five, as the leader of this new movement for Christ.

I asked Fred what he had learned from all of this. "Much" was his short reply. "It's a mystery. God is in control. My job? Trust and obey. Just go, and God is always faithful."

SCHEDULE PRIORITIES

On his final journey to Jerusalem, Jesus spoke to three potential followers about priorities. The first conversation, as we've seen, was about lifestyle priorities.

The second conversation began with Jesus simply telling a man, "Follow me." But for that man, as for most of us, the call of Jesus didn't come at the most convenient time. He replied, "Lord, first let me go and bury my father." You have to admit, the man had a great excuse! As a pastor in my fifth decade of ministry I have heard many "Not now but later" excuses, but none so valid as "Let me bury my dad."

Jesus didn't accept the excuse, no matter how valid. "Let the dead bury their own dead, but you go and proclaim the kingdom of God" (Luke 9:60). In other words, there are plenty of spiritually dead people sitting in pews of churches who can bury each other in their rationalizations, bigotry, and judgmental religion. But we are called to be different, to go and proclaim the kingdom of God in word and deed!

Can you recall a time when your response to a call from God was "Not now but later"? Jesus is calling us to set schedule priorities.

Youth activities can easily become a consuming passion for Christian families, making Jesus a secondary priority. It's all too common for me to hear people say, "We'll be involved again in church after fall soccer." Sadly, these priorities and values are being imprinted into our children's spirits. Our life practices become their lived-out adult priorities.

Remember the important biblical mandate: "Start children off on the way they should go, and even when they are old they will not turn from it" (Proverbs 22:6). Moses reminded the Israelites, in a prayer called the Shema:

41

*Hear, O Israel: The LORD our God, the LORD is one. Love
the LORD your God with all your heart and with all your
soul and with all your strength. These commandments
that I give you today are to be on your hearts. Impress
them on your children. Talk about them when you sit at
home and when you walk along the road, when you lie
down and when you get up. Tie them as symbols on your
hands and bind them on your foreheads. Write them on
the doorframes of your houses and on your gates.*

(Deuteronomy 6:4-9)

Carolyn and I are committed to youth extracurricular activities. We once drove nine hours to Philadelphia to watch our four-year-old granddaughter in a dance recital. Her part lasted all of one minute and fifty-two seconds. Would we do it again? Absolutely! Our son played competitive baseball from age four through Division One college ball. By the seventh grade, weekend tournaments required Sunday morning participation. Fortunately, a Catholic church in our area had a 7:00 a.m. Mass that we had him attend. Why? Training a child in God-first priorities, including schedule priorities, is different from just telling. Both our children are in their thirties, active followers of Jesus, and training their children in the same disciplines.

RELATIONSHIP PRIORITIES

On that final journey to Jerusalem, a third man said to Jesus, "I will follow you, Lord; but first let me go back and say goodbye to my family" (Luke 9:61). This seems to me to be a very valid excuse. The man was willing to follow but made a reasonable request. Jesus didn't agree. He replied, "No one who puts a hand to the plow and looks back is fit for service in the kingdom of God" (v. 62).

In this third response, Jesus was addressing relationship priorities. Many times I've known committed followers of Jesus who compromise that commitment when they become romantically involved with people who are not equally committed. This is what the apostle Paul meant when he wrote,

> *Do not be yoked together with unbelievers.... What*
> *does a believer have in common with an unbeliever?*
> *What agreement is there between the temple of God*
> *and idols? For we are the temple of the living God.*
> *(2 Corinthians 6:14-16)*

We can easily begin to rationalize unequally yoked relationships by telling ourselves that our influence will change the person we are emotionally connected to. For example, I was recently counseling a pre-engaged couple, in which the woman was from a nearby local church. She had become involved with a man whom she had met through a friend. The man had no previous church experience and had been married twice before. The woman had recently discovered that her fiancé was addicted to Internet pornography but believed his promise that he would quit once they were married. Sadly, it didn't work out that way.

Rightly ordering our relationship priorities means:

1. Making sure that our relationship with God is right. This orders all other priorities, responsibilities, and relationships in our lives.
2. Getting my understanding and relationship with myself right. Unless I am aligned with a healthy understanding of myself, I can never be in a healthy relationship with others.
3. Committing to equally yoked, Christ-honoring relationships with others.

When we fail to do the hard work of rightly ordering our relationship priorities, we sometimes seek comfort in past habits and return to easier, less demanding life paths. We mistakenly believe that we can live with a foot in each of two contradictory worlds. But living an abundant life is not about easy. Jesus tells us, "Enter through the narrow gate. For wide is the gate and broad is the road that leads to destruction, and many enter through it. But small is the gate and narrow the road that leads to life, and only a few find it" (Matthew 7:13-14).

Faith is the disciplined act of making relentless commitments to God-honoring activities that result in healthy outcomes.

FRIEND OF SINNERS

As Jesus was nearing Jerusalem in the final days of his journey, he passed through the ancient city of Jericho. Jericho is one of the oldest cities in the world. Archaeologists have discovered remains of settlements that date back to 9000 BC. The abundant springs in the desert area have made it desirable for human habitation through the millennia. Jesus passed through Jericho on numerous occasions. Luke tells us that Jesus first healed a blind beggar sitting alongside the road as he was approaching the city (18:35-43). Next, he encountered Zacchaeus.

Zacchaeus is identified as a wealthy chief tax collector who operated his business in the city of Jericho. First-century tax collectors took in taxes for the hated Roman government. Customs duties were farmed out to Jewish officials, who were willing to extort exorbitant tariffs from the occupied area. These officials, viewed as traitors, were despised by their fellow Jewish neighbors.

Upon hearing of Jesus' arrival in the city, Zacchaeus ran along the crowded streets in an attempt to find the best spot to see him. Luke apparently felt it was important for us to know that Zacchaeus was "short in stature" (Luke 19:3 NRSV). We might assume from this side note that Zacchaeus was dealing with self-esteem issues based on his physical size. I often wonder how many of our life pictures of self and others have been stunted by childhood peers who were quick to point out our personal shortcomings. There are many factors that lead folks such as Zacchaeus into an adulthood of isolation, self-protection, and feelings of inadequacy.

Jesus, immediately sensing Zacchaeus's self-imposed sense of condemnation and isolation, said to him, "Zacchaeus, come down immediately. I must stay at your house today" (v. 5). What a moment! Jesus calls us—broken, selfish people. God knows our name! Take a moment to breathe this truth into your being: you are not just one of eight billion people who inhabit the planet. Say it, along with the psalmist:

> For you created my inmost being;
>> you knit me together in my mother's womb.
> I praise you because I am fearfully and wonderfully made;
>> your works are wonderful,
>> I know that full well.
>
> (Psalm 139:13-14)

Write it down and place it in a spot where you will be frequently reminded of your true identity.

Many religious folks have struggled and continue to struggle with the nature of Jesus' inclusive welcome of sinners into God's kingdom banquet. Along with the people who watched Jesus leave with Zacchaeus, they mutter, "He has gone to be the guest of a sinner" (v. 7). Perhaps the greatest title ever given to Jesus, next to "Son of God," is "friend of sinners." God's miracle through our own life mission occurs when we are willing to be and do the same!

A FINANCIAL COST

The meeting with Zacchaeus came toward the very end of Jesus' earthly ministry, after which his mission would be carried out by his committed followers. As Jesus said, "Very truly I tell you, whoever believes in me will do the works I have been doing, and they will do even greater things than these, because I am going to the Father" (John 14:12).

Zacchaeus immediately grasped the financial obligation that came with accepting Jesus' invitation. He proclaimed, "Look, Lord! Here and now I give half of my possessions to the poor, and if I have cheated anybody out of anything, I will pay back four times the amount" (Luke 19:8).

Today, we would do well to follow the example of Zacchaeus. The sad truth is that Americans are being held captive by a culture of consumption. Our celebration of Thanksgiving is interwoven with Black Friday (nothing resembling Good Friday), closely followed by Small Business Saturday and Cyber Monday. Debt has become a way of life for the majority of us. In 2016, a study of American household credit card debt revealed the indebtedness of the average American household:

- Credit card debt: $16,748
- Mortgages: $176,222
- Auto loans: $28,948
- Student loans: $49,905
- Average amount owed by American households with debt: A staggering $134,643![3]

As Christians, we are in danger of the same fiscal paralysis that infected the church of Laodicea mentioned in Revelation 3:15-17.

*I know your deeds, that you are neither cold nor hot. I
wish you were either one or the other! So, because you
are lukewarm—neither hot nor cold—I am about to
spit you out of my mouth. You say, "I am rich; I have
acquired wealth and do not need a thing." But you do
not realize that you are wretched, pitiful, poor, blind
and naked.*

Zacchaeus understood clearly that true repentance is
demonstrated in the reordering of our financial priorities. Jesus
affirmed Zacchaeus's actions as a visible sign of transformation:
"Today salvation has come to this house, because this man, too, is
a son of Abraham. For the Son of Man came to seek and to save
what was lost" (Luke 19: 9-10).

Miracles come with a cost. When Jesus told his disciples that
the impending hour of his sacrifice had come, he also reminded
them, "Very truly I tell you, unless a kernel of wheat falls to the
ground and dies, it remains only a single seed. But if it dies, it
produces many seeds." He went on to remind them, and us:
"Whoever serves me must follow me; and where I am, my servant
will also be" (John 12:24, 26).

Where is Jesus today? We experience him in the world's hungry,
the thirsty, the immigrant, the naked, and the prisoner. "Truly I tell
you," said Jesus, "whatever you did for one of the least of these
brothers and sisters of mine, you did for me" (Matthew 25:40).

Serving Jesus is both costly and sacrificial. We are not saved
to wait passively for heaven but to be the channels through which
God's miraculous resources are released on earth. Yes, at times it
will hurt. Even Jesus prayed for the Father to deliver him from his
painful mission. "Now my soul is troubled, and what shall I say?
'Father save me from this hour'? No, it was for this very reason that
I came to this hour. Father, glorify your name!" (John 12:27-28).

47

Now is the time to assess the cost you are willing to incur to prepare yourself for experiencing God's miracles in and through your life. This may mean eliminating a habit, removing a distraction, or simplifying a lifestyle. It may also mean beginning a new life practice or strategy for reprioritizing the mandates and miracles of God in your life. Following are a few starting point ideas for consideration.

REFLECTION

What costs are you willing to incur in order to more fully experience God's miracles in and through your life? Here are some possibilities:

- Eliminate unnecessary spending, avoiding the siren call of the Internet ads, Facebook promotions, or storefront displays that promise happiness through materialism.

- Impose and adhere to a daily time limit on social media. Use the saved time to spend more time in the Word, calling a friend, or engaging in hands-and-feet mission. Turn screen time into walk time.

- Practice moderation in your eating habits. Keep your body, God's temple, in its best condition for lifelong health, wellness, and mission.

- Begin putting your finances in order. Does your church or a church near you offer programs in personal financial management and stewardship? These programs have been completely transformational in the lives of many Ginghamsburg families. Remember, your resources are not your own.

- Invest in key relationships. Resolve to handwrite notes of encouragement or thankfulness to people you love who have invested in your life in a meaningful way.

- Join that small group you have been thinking about.

- Spend drive time as prayer time, turning off the music, podcast, or audio book.

- Relook at the family calendar. Where have you been failing to prioritize God as a family? What will you remove, reschedule, or simplify?

Miracles come with a cost. But, the payoff can truly be amazing—and eternal.

3
THE MIRACLE OF LOVE

3

THE MIRACLE OF LOVE

"My command is this: Love each other as I have loved you. Greater love has no one than this: to lay down one's life for one's friends."

(John 15:12-13)

It has been said that the two most difficult things to get straight in life are love and God. More often than not, the mess that people make of their lives can be traced to failure or stupidity in one or both. Jesus reminds us that the practices of loving God, self, and others are intricately linked together. You can't truly love others if you don't love yourself, nor will you truly be able to love yourself apart from experiencing God's immeasurable love for you.

During Jesus' life on earth he only left his followers with one new commandment that equaled the sum total of all of the law and prophets: "A new command I give you: Love one another. As I have loved you, so you must love one another. By this everyone will know that you are my disciples, if you love one another" (John 13:34-35). Did you catch the phrase "As I have loved you"? Jesus is the visible demonstration on earth of the essence of God's nature. Jesus is God in the flesh who touches untouchables, loves enemies, eats with sinners, and takes the punishment upon himself that's due for us who are guilty. God is love!

God has a loving plan for each of us. Every action of Jesus is motivated by God's unfailing love. Jesus reminds us that no need is too small or inconsequential for God's concern about our well-being: "Your Father knows what you need before you ask him" (Matthew 6:8).

Do you want to be encouraged? Take a moment and search through your web browser for scriptures about God's love.

GOD IS LOVE

Everyone who loves has been born of God and knows God. Whoever does not love does not know God, because God is love.

(1 John 4:7b-8)

Pondering God and God's miracles presents us with an opportunity to examine and rightly order our love priorities. We sin when our loves are out of order. God loved everything into being. Love is the foundation of creation. Love is the driving force behind every miracle. God is a God of relationships, as demonstrated in the relationship of the Holy Trinity.

Pastor Jonathan Marlowe described the relationship of the three persons of the Trinity as "the dance of love":

The theologians in the early church tried to describe this wonderful reality that we call Trinity. If any of you have ever been to a Greek wedding, you may have seen their distinctive way of dancing. . . . It's called perichoresis. There are not two dancers, but at least three. They start to go in circles, weaving in and out in this very beautiful pattern of motion. They start to go faster and faster and faster, all the while staying in perfect rhythm and in sync with each other. Eventually, they are dancing so quickly (yet so effortlessly) that as you look at them, it just becomes a blur. Their individual identities are part of a larger dance. The early church fathers and mothers looked at that dance (perichoresis) and said, "That's what the Trinity is like." It's a harmonious set of relationship in which there is mutual giving and receiving. This relationship is called love, and it's what the Trinity is all about. The perichoresis is the dance of love.[1]

Relationship is the essence of Trinity. You and I are created to be in the life rhythm of this holy dance of communion with God and one another. Everything begins with our own understanding of God's unfailing, unconditional love.

HOW DO YOU PICTURE GOD?

Your picture of God determines how you perceive yourself and others. Many of us have a picture of God other than the merciful Father who "demonstrates his own love for us in this: While we were still sinners, Christ died for us" (Romans 5:8). Bad theology through the millennia has created images of cultural deities that support humanity's worst characteristics.

A God of Wrath and Vengeance

Some picture a god of wrath and vengeance who demands "an eye for an eye and a tooth for a tooth." Jesus challenged misrepresentations of God's character found in some of the culturally bound images in the Old Testament: "You have heard that it was said, 'Eye for eye, and tooth for tooth' But I tell you, do not resist an evil person. If anyone slaps you on the right cheek, turn to them the other cheek also" (Matthew 5:38-39). Jesus goes on in this same passage to direct his followers to "love your enemies and pray for those who persecute you" (v. 44).

We must learn to discern biblical truth through the life and teachings of Jesus and not blindly hold every text as representing the character and will of God. The books of Leviticus and Deuteronomy, for example, talk about marriage violations. If a woman did not satisfy her husband that she was by proof a virgin on the night of their marriage,

> she shall be brought to the door of her father's house
> and there the men of her town shall stone her to death.
> She has done an outrageous thing in Israel by being
> promiscuous while still in her father's house. You must
> purge the evil from among you.
>
> (Deuteronomy 22:21)

This barbaric practice is still being carried out in some countries. A Pakistani woman named Samia Sarwar was murdered in her lawyer's office by an assassin hired by her parents, who felt that she had brought shame to the family because of adultery.[2]

How radically different was the love that Jesus showed the woman caught in the act of adultery when the men of her village were ready to commit the same murderous act. Jesus intervened, saying, "Let any one of you who is without sin be the first to throw a stone at her" (John 8:7) Wow! We are all guilty. But thank God that God loves sinners!

At this, those who heard began to go away one at a time, the older ones first, until only Jesus was left, with the woman still standing there. Jesus straightened up and asked her, "Woman, where are they? Has no one condemned you?"

"No one, sir," she said.

"Then neither do I condemn you," Jesus declared. "Go now and leave your life of sin."

(John 8:9-11)

Forgiveness precedes life change! God's loving acceptance becomes the motive for change and is in no way connected to our personal successes or failures. Jesus reveals God as a loving father who comes into the world not to condemn but to save sinners!

An Ancient White Male

Other people view God as an ancient white male, as portrayed in medieval European paintings. Michelangelo's painting of the Creation of Adam (1508–12), which covers part of the Sistine Chapel ceiling, is just one example.

All kinds of atrocities have emerged from this distortion: racism and the injustices committed in the name of ethnic superiority, as well as sexist discrimination, continuing in some religious circles, that excludes women from leadership. In the United States, women continue to be paid 20 percent less than men for doing equal work. By contrast, early first-century Jesus followers discovered the miraculous, unifying love of God in which "there is neither Jew nor Gentile, neither slave nor free, nor is there male and female, for you are all one in Christ Jesus" (Galatians 3:28).

A Tribal God

The current rabid division in US politics, as well as in much of the Christian church, can result from a picture of a god who is tribal, a god who is "for us and against the people we are against." Author Anne Lamott gives an excellent example of this misrepresentation: "You can safely assume that you created God in your own image when it turns out that God hates all the same people you hate."[3] Historians will identify the post-9/11 environment as an age of anxiety. Fear is an irrational emotion based on current circumstances or perceived future events. The 2016 presidential election demonstrated a growing sense of isolationism based on the fear of terrorism. Building walls that would keep people out became the mantra. In the early spring of 2017, there were a growing number of threats made against Jewish communities and Muslim mosques. Jewish cemeteries were vandalized. Two Indian businessmen were shot in Kansas, while the perpetrator shouted, "Get out of my country!"[4] The following August, deadly violence erupted at a white nationalist rally in Charlottesville, Virginia, leaving one woman dead and nineteen people injured while fueling fear and reopening racial divides within the United States.[5] The apostle Paul also spoke about walls in describing Jesus:

> *For he himself is our peace, who has made the two groups one and has destroyed the barrier, the dividing wall of hostility. . . . His purpose was to create in himself one new humanity out of the two, thus making peace, and in one body to reconcile both of them to God through the cross, by which he put to death their hostility. He came and preached peace to you who were far away and peace to those who were near. For through him we both have access to the Father by one Spirit.*
>
> *(Ephesians 2:14-18)*

God's love is the miraculous healing force that tears down the walls that divide us.

God of the Nation-State

Closely related to the god of the tribe is the god of the nation-state. Constantine, who ruled the Roman Empire in AD 306–337, saw how the strength of the early Christian movement could unify and legitimize Rome's dominance as the global power. It's pretty safe to assume that Constantine's legalization of Christianity had a deep, underlying political motive, uniting the flag of Rome with the symbol of Christ. This is not unlike flying the Christian flag under the American flag.

The god of the nation-state holds one nation favored above all others. One such example today is the Islamic state; past examples include the millennia of wars fought in the name of God. Israel forgot that its chosen status, described in Exodus 19:6, was not for privilege but for priesthood. God promised Abraham that "through your offspring all nations on earth will be blessed…" (Genesis 22:18). We must never forget "that God so loved the world"!

Cosmic Traffic Cop

Your dominant picture of God might be as the cosmic traffic cop or courtroom judge. What do you do when you're cruising down the expressway and see a state trooper holding a radar gun? My immediate instinct is to hit my brakes, even if I'm doing the speed limit. You probably agree with me in the need for law enforcement, but all the same, we want to avoid law enforcement in our daily travel routes.

The one exception is when we experience an emergency crisis. How many people who view God this way feel that they can handle the majority of daily living on their own and turn to God only in times of dire need?

WHY JESUS?

The Word became flesh and blood,
and moved into the neighborhood.
We saw the glory with our own eyes,
the one-of-a-kind glory,
like Father, like Son,
Generous inside and out,
true from start to finish.
(John 1:14 MSG)

My friend and mentor Will Willimon continues to help me connect with the core meaning of the Jesus event. Will writes,

> God is not whom we expected. We thought we knew what is indicated by "God," then Jesus showed up as "the way, the truth, and the life" the only way to the Father (Jn. 14:6), and we had to rearrange our ideas about God once we got a good look at who God really is—a Jew on a cross, arms outstretched in love of people who don't love him.[6]

As we follow Jesus' life and teaching, we experience God's true identity. We have a living picture of who God is and what God values. No longer is God merely a philosophical idea for systematic theologians to debate about. In Jesus, we experience God who values human relationships over legalistic doctrines and people over ideologies.

Bible idolatry is one of the heresies plaguing the church today. The Bible is authoritative and inspired for faith and life practice. We begin to cross the line into heresy however, when we idolize the Scriptures (written word) over Jesus' authority (Living Word).

The totality of God's revelation cannot be limited to the 1,113 pages in my Bible but can be fully discovered in the miraculous transforming love of God revealed in Jesus.

Jesus confronted this idolatry when he challenged the legalists of his day: "You study the Scriptures diligently because you think that in them you have eternal life. These are the very Scriptures that testify about me" (John 5:39). The first disciples of Jesus found a greater life truth in the Living Word. The author of the First Epistle of John writes: "That which was from the beginning, which we have heard, which we have seen with our eyes, which we have looked at and our hands have touched—this we proclaim concerning the Word of life" (1 John 1:1).

Critics challenged Jesus for not following Sabbath rules. Jesus reminded them that rules are not necessarily absolute. Human well-being is what counts! "The sabbath was made for humankind, and not humankind for the sabbath; so the Son of Man is lord even of the sabbath" (Mark 2:27-28 NRSV).

The Samaritans were despised by the Jews because of their distorted practice of Judaism and mixed ancestry. Yet Jesus turned the divisive doctrine upside down in his parable of the good Samaritan (Luke 10:25-37). What's the point? It's that sacrificial demonstrations of love trump rigidly held beliefs. The apostle Paul addressed the doctrinal divide found in the church in Galatia: "For in Christ Jesus neither circumcision nor uncircumcision has any value. The only thing that matters is faith expressing itself through love" (Galatians 5:6).

Far too many people believe that conversion is to an agreed-upon set of doctrinal beliefs. Beliefs are important. My whole life is based on my belief in the physical resurrection of Jesus from the grave. But Jesus calls us to follow in a life path that leads beyond a set of beliefs to a compassionate, loving, serving way of life.

The Samaritan woman Jesus met at the well wanted to hide her own brokenness behind the cloaked wall of theological debate. In John 4:22-24, Jesus responded by essentially saying to the woman, "Your theology about correct and incorrect liturgical practice, places of worship, and theories on the atonement are not what ultimately matters" (my paraphrase). In Jesus' own words, what ultimately matters is this: "God is spirit, and his worshipers must worship in the Spirit and truth" (v. 24).

People who try to live truth without the Spirit, in a stance of judgmental exclusion, become toxins in God's redemptive purpose for the world. Jesus reminded us in the Sermon on the Mount that God's love is indiscriminate: "But I tell you, love your enemies and pray for those who persecute you, that you may be children of your Father in heaven. He causes his sun to rise on the evil and the good, and sends rain on the righteous and the unrighteous" (Matthew 5:44-46).

GOD OF THE PARTY

As Jesus continued his fateful journey to Jerusalem, recorded in the Gospel of Luke, he reminded the folks along the way of God's unfailing love for lost, broken people. Jesus shed light on God's redemptive love by telling three parables that we can read in Luke 15: the stories of the lost sheep, the lost coin, and the lost brothers.

In the lost sheep story, the good shepherd leaves the ninety-nine sheep that are safely in the fold to go after the one who is lost until he finds it, then "joyfully puts it on his shoulders and goes home" (vv. 5-6).

In the lost coin story, a woman becomes obsessed with one lost coin. She turns her house upside down until she finds it. (I've been known to exhibit the same obsessive behavior when trying to find my misplaced cell phone or car keys.)

Now let's zero in on the third parable, the one often called the parable of the prodigal son but which I like to call the lost brothers. The younger son asks for his share of the father's inheritance. How would you feel if you were his dad—being asked before you passed? Obviously the son shows indifference and disregard for the concerns of his father. If the son had a tattoo, I imagine it would have been a dollar sign!

Next, the son chooses to establish an identity apart from his father by moving to "a distant country" (v. 13). While there, he abandons his family identity and "squandered his wealth in wild living." Many college students have done the same. They leave home, find a crowd where they can fit in, and under pressure from their peers do what would be unthinkable in the past.

At some point the younger son begins to realize that his life plan isn't working and his life has become unmanageable.

> *"When he came to his senses, he said, 'How many of*
> *my father's hired servants have food to spare, and here*
> *I am starving to death! I will set out and go back to my*
> *father and say to him: Father, I have sinned against*
> *heaven and against you. I am no longer worthy to*
> *be called your son; make me like one of your hired*
> *servants.' So he got up and went to his father."*
>
> *(vv. 17-19)*

This next part is my favorite:

> *"But while he was still a long way off, his father saw*
> *him and was filled with compassion for him; he ran to*
> *his son, threw his arms around him and kissed him."*
>
> *(v. 20)*

What a father! What a God! Before we find our way back even close to where we should be, God runs to us, has compassion for us, and throws his arms around us. Then he prepares the party of all parties for the son who has returned home safely.

That's the parable of the prodigal son. But remember, I prefer to call it the parable of the lost brothers, because there were two sons, not one. And this is where the older brother enters the picture.

When the younger son returns, his older brother refuses to participate in the feast. The older son points out that he has stayed home, "slaving" for his father, while the younger son has "squandered" the father's love and provision.

The older son finds his identity in legalism and judgmentalism, which have created an emotional and relational distance from his father: "Look! All these years I've been slaving for you and never disobeyed your orders" (v. 29). He views the relationship with the father as being based on his ability to perform rather than living in the security of a beloved child.

How many of us are missing the party because of a distorted understanding of God's nature, God's relationship with us, and God's commitment to us? To participate in the party, all we have to do is ask. As Jesus put it,

> "Ask and it will be given to you; seek and you will find; knock and the door will be open to you. For everyone who asks receives; the one who seeks finds; and to the one who knocks, the door will be opened.
>
> "Which of you if your son asks for bread will give him a stone? Or if he asks for a fish will you give him a snake? If you, then, though you are evil, know how to give good gifts to your children, how much more will your Father in heaven give good gifts to those who ask him! So in

everything, do to others what you would have them do
to you, for this sums up the Law and the Prophets."

(Matthew 7:7-12)

OUR MISSION: BRINGING GOD'S PARTY
TO THE NEIGHBORHOOD

God loves parties! Our salvation is not rooted in a system of beliefs but in a God who throws open the doors to a banquet feast.

Again and again in the Gospels, Jesus talks about banquets. In Matthew 22, he begins a parable by saying, "The kingdom of heaven is like a king who prepared a wedding banquet for his son. He sent his servants to those who had been invited to the banquet to tell them to come, but they refused to come" (vv. 2-3).

As a result, like those of us who get distracted in the details of daily life, many of the invited guests missed the party. But the banquet was ready, and the king wanted guests. He told his servants,

> *"'Go to the street corners and invite to the banquet any-*
> *one you find.' So the servants went out in the streets and*
> *gathered all the people they could find, the bad as well as*
> *the good, and the wedding hall was filled with guests."*
>
> *(vv. 9-10)*

Hold on! The bad as well as the good? Bring the riff-raff, the burn-outs, the drunks, gays, straights, anyone and everyone! Does this look anything like the faith community where you belong?

The next part of this story is critical and yet easy to misconstrue.

> *"But when the king came in to see the guests, he noticed*
> *a man there who was not wearing wedding clothes.*
> *He asked, 'How did you get in here without wedding*
> *clothes, friend?' The man was speechless.*

*"Then the king told the attendants, 'Tie him hand and
foot, and throw him outside, into the darkness, where
there will be weeping and gnashing of teeth.'*

"For many are invited, but few are chosen."

(vv. 11-14)

Ready for the surprise twist? Who was the one not dressed
appropriately in wedding clothes? It would be easy to assume it was
someone of questionable reputation or misguided faith. Maybe it's
your Muslim next-door neighbor. It could be the argumentative
atheist in your building whom you try to avoid whenever possible.
Could it be the lesbian couple who sat down in the pew beside you
last week in church? Or the man sitting in front of you who has
been divorced four times?

But as the apostle Paul reminded the Christians in Galatia, "So
in Christ Jesus you are all children of God through faith, for all of
you who were baptized into Christ have clothed yourselves with
Christ" (Galatians 3:26-27).

That's it—clothed in Christ! We are to be dressed in the mind
of Christ, in the love of Christ, clothed and committed to carrying
out the mission of Christ!

Which means, Paul continued, "There is neither Jew nor
Gentile, neither slave nor free, nor is there male and female, for
you are all one in Christ Jesus" (v. 28).

Our mission is not to judge but to bring God's party to both the
bad and the good in the neighborhood.

PERFORMING MIRACLES OF LOVE

Radwa Sobieh is all about breaking down the barriers that
divide. Radwa is a busy mom of two girls and a practicing dentist in
northern Virginia. She was also the only Muslim member of a recent

Ginghamsburg medical missions team that traveled to Jamaica to host medical clinics in partnership with an organization known as American-Caribbean Experience (ACE). This was actually Radwa's third trip to Jamaica to serve with ACE. When I asked Radwa how she had learned about the Ginghamsburg trips to Jamaica, she replied that Anna, one of the attending dentists at a Dayton-area hospital where Radwa did her residency, had remained Radwa's Facebook friend post-residency. Anna was active not only on Facebook but also in mission, frequently posting photos of her own excursions to serve in Jamaica. When Radwa contacted Anna asking for details of how to get involved, Anna forwarded the paperwork.

Radwa says, "That's when I knew that the organization she traveled with was affiliated with Ginghamsburg Church. Not for a moment did I have a change of heart or consider backing out. I did not see a difference between a church, a mosque, or a synagogue! We are all humans helping other humans and working toward the same goal at the end. My only problem was that I didn't know if those working on the mission trip would share that same belief. So I called Anna and asked for her opinion."

Radwa reports that the conversation was as simple as this:

> Radwa: Hey Anna, so I see you travel with a church. Do you think they will have a problem with me going since you know I'm Muslim and stuff?
>
> Anna: No, they won't have a problem. Do you have a problem traveling with them?
>
> Radwa: Of course not!

"And that was it," Radwa said.

I asked Radwa what convinced her, a busy professional, to leave her daughters and dental practice behind for a week at a time to serve in Jamaica. She told me, "I remember when the Japanese tsunami and earthquake happened in 2011; I was watching the news with one of my daughters who was seven at the time. We were both moved to tears and devastated seeing actual footage of the destruction, the suffering, and the deaths it left behind. After watching the news, my daughter looked at me and said. 'Mommy, what are we going to do?' My plan was to go about with my day as usual, but her question was so direct and simple. She sounded like we had no choice but to do something, and she was right! I looked at her and said, 'We are going to pray for them and their country and go online on the Red Cross website and donate money right now.' And that's exactly what we did."

Radwa added, "When I see or hear about new disasters, illnesses, poor living conditions all around the world, now I feel an urge to help out in any way I can. It's like I imagine God asking me directly, 'So maybe you didn't have a hand in the suffering that's going on, but what did you do to help alleviate it?'" That question and Anna's photos led her to Jamaica medical missions.

After Radwa returned from her most recent Jamaica excursion, she posted several Facebook entries about the trip. She described her experience online, of course, but also used it as a platform to appeal to others, including fellow Muslims, to get involved in serving the needs of the world.

She wrote, "Please get out there and be involved in your communities; help out and volunteer in any way you can. It is great to volunteer in the mosque, but it is also as important to volunteer in your community, to join Boy Scouts, to get to know your neighbors, to coach your kids' soccer team, to give back to the people and the place you are blessed to live in."

Radwa also encouraged readers, "Explain that you are doing it because this is what your religion tells you to do. You will see the change happening in front of your eyes. You will see people who were skeptical about you and your practices become your best friends and even your advocates."

Radwa also shared on Facebook how much she enjoyed being part of a team in which artificial barriers were set aside—profession, age, religion, race. Team meant team. "I have a picture of five doctors making sandwiches for everybody. Everyone carried the furniture and supplies to and from the buses to set up the clinic. No one complained of the heat, the harsh working conditions, or the long days. Indeed, we are all God's servants. Let's act like it."

In northern Virginia (Metro DC) where Radwa lives, she witnesses frequent interfaith collaboration, and loves it. "Inviting others to your place of worship creates a special bond; opening up to one another defeats misconceptions and alienation. In praying together, we realize that we all have the same goals, needs, and worries and can serve humanity together."

As Radwa concluded on Facebook after her trip, "Love always brings love."

I say, "Amen."

God is the source of love. Love is not something we can ever manufacture. We need it, and we complete it. As the apostle John points out, "Since God so loved us, we also ought to love one another. No one has ever seen God; but if we love one another, God lives in us and his love is made complete in us" (1 John 4:11-12).

What is love ultimately? It's the perfect intersection of divine intervention with human initiative—the stuff that miracles are made of.

REFLECTION

How can you be the visible demonstration of the miracle of God's love? Here are a few thought-starters.

- Open up your home to neighbors with an open-table meal or a "y'all come and bring a side dish" night.

- Identify an opportunity to host or participate in a barrier-busting event within your community. What part can you play in a real and tangible way to bring people together across racial, socioeconomic, political, or religious divides for conversation or a common cause?

- Sign up for a mission experience. Don't have the money or time to take a trip? Serve each Saturday at a shelter, food pantry, or soup kitchen. Contact organizations that serve local refugee populations, and see how you can be a part. (One good starting point is often Catholic Social Services.) Tutor kids over your lunch hour at your nearest neighborhood school.

- Hold or join an ecumenical prayer meeting for your community.

4

ACTIVATE THE POWER
OF FAITH

4

ACTIVATE THE POWER OF FAITH

Now on his way to Jerusalem, Jesus traveled along the border between Samaria and Galilee. As he was going into a village, ten men who had leprosy met him. They stood at a distance and called out in a loud voice, "Jesus, Master, have pity on us!"

When he saw them, he said, "Go, show yourselves to the priest." And as they went, they were cleansed.

(Luke 17:11-14)

The tendency for many of us is to reduce faith to intellectual affirmation of a doctrinal position (such as the declaration of faith outlined in the Apostles' Creed) or to view true faith as the absence of doubt. I have shared with folks on numerous occasions my own intellectual struggles with faith. My whole adult life focus has been committed to the historical reality of the resurrection of Jesus Christ. I live my life and expend my resources based on this biblical claim.

But if truth be told, empty tombs are irrational. They don't align with human experience. I have never seen or heard of any credible evidence documenting a physical resurrection from the grave since that first-century account. But true faith is not the absence of doubt, nor is it dependent on empirical scientific proof.

I BELIEVE; HELP MY UNBELIEF

A man brought Jesus his son, who had been suffering from the symptoms of epileptic seizures. The man said,

> *"Teacher, I brought you my son, who is possessed by a spirit that has robbed him of speech. Whenever it seizes him, it throws him to the ground. He foams at the mouth, gnashes his teeth and becomes rigid. I asked your disciples to drive out the spirit, but they could not. . . . But if you can do anything, take pity on us and help him."*
>
> *" 'If you can'?" said Jesus. "Everything is possible for one who believes."*
>
> (Mark 9:17-18, 22-23)

Everything? Yes, that is exactly what Jesus said! Here comes the part of the conversation that has become my personal prayer for the last four-plus decades. "Immediately the boy's father exclaimed, 'I do believe; help me overcome my unbelief!'" (v. 24).

If your struggle is similar to mine, I invite you to make this prayer a part of your daily faith journey: "I do believe; help me overcome my unbelief!"

As we continue our faith journey, we encounter Jesus' own personal struggle in tension with faith and, at the same time, an overwhelming sense of God's absence. Now, before you call that last statement heretical, take a moment to consider the full humanness of Jesus. Far too many times we embrace the divinity of Jesus but forget that he was fully human at the same time. Paul reminded the church in Philippi that Jesus,

> *being in very nature God,*
> *did not consider equality with God something to be*
> *used to his own advantage;*
> *rather, he made himself nothing*
> *by taking the very nature of a servant,*
> *being made in human likeness.*
>
> *(Philippians 2: 6-7)*

It is impossible to fully grasp the events surrounding the Easter event without embracing the full humanity of Jesus. Like all human beings, Jesus grew in his understanding of God, faith, and his own life mission. He was tempted and experienced pain and suffering, just like you and me. Jesus experienced the same wide range of emotions—doubt, fear, joy, laughter, sadness—that all human beings experience.

As a matter of fact, Jesus was so ordinarily human that those closest to him struggled with his messianic claims. "Is this not Jesus, the son of Joseph, whose father and mother we know? How can he now say, 'I came down from heaven?'" (John 6:42). The Gospel writer goes on to remind us, "Even his own brothers did not believe in him" (7:5).

A FULLY HUMAN MESSIAH

Enter with me into the anguish of Jesus' personal struggle, as he left the upper room following his celebration of the Passover with his disciples and walked across the Kidron Valley to the Mount of Olives.

He prayed, "Father, if you are willing, take this cup from me; yet not my will, but yours be done" (Luke 22:42). Feel the tension between all-out faith and retreat! "And being in anguish, he prayed more earnestly, and his sweat was like drops of blood falling to the ground" (v. 44).

Jesus came to the point of feeling totally forsaken by God, in utter humiliation and pain in the last moments before his death. "My God, my God, why have you forsaken me?" (Matthew 27:46). Yet Luke reminds us that these feelings of God's absence did not prohibit Jesus' last expression of faith.

> It was now about noon, and darkness came over the whole land until three in the afternoon, for the sun stopped shining. And the curtain of the temple was torn in two. Jesus called out with a loud voice, "Father, into your hands I commit my spirit." When he had said this, he breathed his last.
>
> (Luke 23:44-46)

Where are you, God? Why, God? These are the questions all of us ask in hours of darkness, when it seems as if the sun has stopped shining.

I am writing this chapter during the week when one of the worst chemical bombings in Syria has turned a rebel-held northern area into a toxic kill zone. I'm looking at pictures of parents carrying their lifeless children and at images of the bodies of civilians lying in streets where they collapsed from proximity to the deadly vapor.

Why, God?

A few days ago during Palm Sunday services, ISIS attacked two Coptic Orthodox churches in Egypt's Nile Delta, killing more than forty people and injuring more than one hundred others.

How can this be allowed to happen, God?

A thirteen-year-old boy died this week from a heroin overdose, attributed to his parents' own use in the home.

Where are you, God?

Jesus' last words on the cross began with a reminder of who God is: Father. God is not distant and uninvolved. God is an all-out, all-in, all-consumed infinite parent. God is unconditional and perfect love, love without limits. If you are a parent or grandparent, you know exactly what Jesus meant in that one simple word. There is nothing that most of us would not do or give up for the well-being of our children and grandchildren, including our own lives. Our children might not always understand it, but it is nevertheless true that we are always acting for their best and doing our best, in spite of our human limitations.

How much more, God?

Jesus reminds us, "Which of you, if your son asks for bread, will give him a stone? Or if he asks for a fish, will give him a snake? If you, then, though you are evil, know how to give good gifts to your children, how much more will your Father in heaven give good gifts to those who ask him!" (Matthew 7:9-11).

Faith, as Jesus demonstrated on the cross, is feeling fear and still trusting God's absolute love in spite of it: "Father, into your hands I commit my spirit" (Luke 23:46).

In Jesus' feeling of overwhelming darkness and sense of forsakenness, he clung to the promise of Scripture. His last words directly quote Psalm 31:5: "Into your hands I commit my spirit; deliver me, LORD, my faithful God." Luke omits the second part of this verse, but its meaning would have been deeply embedded in Jesus' consciousness. In spite of feeling forsakenness and overwhelming darkness, Jesus trusted that God would ultimately redeem him and turn the darkness to light.

WHO DO YOU SAY THAT I AM?

You might be struggling to truly understand who the person of Jesus is. Prophet? Jewish sage? Galilean rebel? Son of God?

Scott is a good friend of mine who identified himself as an agnostic when we first met. I encouraged Scott to study and to begin to apply the teachings of Jesus in his daily life. No pressure, no hurry. Begin to practice Jesus' teachings and see where it would lead. After all, the journey of faith is progressive.

We find an account in the Gospel of John where Jesus healed a man in a most unusual manner.

> *He spit on the ground, made some mud with the saliva,*
> *and put it on the man's eyes. "Go," he told him, "wash*
> *in the Pool of Siloam."... So the man went and washed,*
> *and came home seeing.*
>
> *(John 9:6-7)*

This encounter is a great example of a miracle resulting from a divine directive and a corresponding human action. Even after such an extraordinary experience of transformation, the man confessed his ignorance in understanding the theological dynamics of Jesus' identity. The man said simply, "Whether he is a sinner or not, I don't know. One thing I do know. I was blind but now I see!" (v. 25). My friend Scott now identifies himself as a "tentative Christian."

The disciples had been following Jesus for some time before he ever put to them the question, "Who do you say I am?" (Matthew 16:15). There was still some uncertainty among Jesus' admiring crowds. "Some say John the Baptist; others say Elijah; and still others, Jeremiah or one of the prophets" (v. 14). Simon Peter, however, was able to make the bold profession of faith at this juncture. "You are the Messiah, the Son of the living God" (v. 16).

ACTING ON GOD'S DIRECTIVE

I struggle with faith but have experienced faith's supernatural results in my life and ministry when I dare to act on God's directive. There is a difference between belief and faith. Belief is holding to an opinion or conviction; faith is the commitment to respond to that conviction by taking a course of action. Jesus doesn't need more fans. Jesus is calling us to risk acting on the irrationality of resurrection claims in order to experience the miracles of resurrection realities.

At the beginning of this chapter, we read a passage from Luke describing the ten men with leprosy who were healed by Jesus. Note that the men were not healed solely on the basis of their request. They were healed when they acted: "as they went, they were cleansed" (Luke 17:14). One of the men took this miraculous intervention a step further: "He threw himself at Jesus' feet and thanked him—and he was a Samaritan" (v. 16).

We mentioned in a previous chapter that the Samaritans were considered by the Jews to have a heretical theology and compromised genealogy. But this man, who may not have been able to pass a theological exam, put himself in the place of humble servitude at Jesus' feet. He didn't receive, forget, and go on with his life as usual. The miracle changed his life direction and purpose. Jesus told the man that a deeper miracle of healing had transpired: "Rise and go; your faith has made you well" (v. 19).

The other nine men were "cleansed" of the outward symptoms of their physical disease, but this man was transformed in the wholeness of his being. The Greek word for *well* used in this text is often translated as "has saved you," indicating that miracles have a deeper underlying purpose that goes beyond temporal needs. This is why the miracles of Jesus are called "signs" in the Gospel of John. The "signs" point to a more profound reality found in the person of Jesus:

> *Jesus performed many other signs in the presence of his disciples, which are not recorded in this book. But these are written that you may believe that Jesus is the Messiah, the Son of God, and that by believing you may have life in his name.*

> *(John 20:30-31)*

As the ten lepers so clearly illustrated, miracles are activated through obedience in action, not just belief.

RISKING FORWARD

The story that follows the feeding of the five thousand in Matthew 14 is another perfect example. After the leftovers had been collected following the hillside feast of bread and fish, Jesus withdrew again for prayer and solitude, directing his disciples in his absence to board the boat and set sail across the Sea of Galilee for the next destination. As we soon find out, however, it was not exactly smooth sailing.

When the boat was "a considerable distance from land" (v. 24), stormy seas and wind began buffeting the boat, and Jesus was not on board to offer encouragement. The stage was set for Peter to do something remarkable that would demonstrate the true difference between belief and faith. As Peter demonstrated, there are three key actions of faith: risking forward, failing forward, and praying forward.

As the disciples struggled to make forward progress in the tumultuous seas, they noticed a figure walking toward them on the water ahead. It was Jesus! All except Peter cried out in fear, believing it to be a ghost. Their response wasn't surprising. After all, fear is part of our ancestral DNA, an innate response connected to our sense of survival. Fear can be helpful, reminding us to stay in secure, safe places, avoiding danger and risk. However, fear can also be a barrier to the risking forward required to follow Jesus. Peter was about to experience the extraordinary only available to us when we risk forward in faith.

> But Jesus immediately said to them: "Take courage! It is I. Don't be afraid."
>
> "Lord, if it's you," Peter replied, "tell me to come to you on the water."
>
> "Come," he said.
>
> Then Peter got down out of the boat, walked on the water and came toward Jesus.
>
> (Matthew 14:27-29)

Faith requires us to leave the safe and predictable, instead risking out into unknown and sometimes uncomfortable places. Actions of faith often don't seem rational at the times we need to take them. In 1979, when I was a twenty-seven-year-old pastor with a young family, it wasn't rational to leave my role as a youth pastor in a "country club" church in my hometown of Cincinnati and head to the little semirural town of Ginghamsburg to lead a resistant congregation of ninety. But if Carolyn and I had not taken that risk, look at the nearly forty years of blessings and miracles we would have missed out on!

Faith requires obedience, and obedience initiates God's power. In Paul's letter to the Hebrews, he lifts up Abraham as the father of faith: "By faith Abraham, when called to go to a place he would later receive as his inheritance, obeyed and went, even though he did not know where he was going" (Hebrews 11:8).

Interestingly, Abraham may have been powerful in faith, but he was actually marginal in belief. Abraham had no Bible, no temple, and no concept of heaven or hell to fall back on. He was part of a polytheistic culture. But Abraham's obedience activated God's power and eventually would set the world on course to launch three major religions: Judaism, Christianity, and Islam.

As noted previously, the four Gospels show Jesus saying "Follow me" 87 times and "believe in me" just twice. The words *worship me* never appear. The term *Christian* is used 3 times in the New Testament, whereas *disciple*, one who follows, appears more than 250 times.

Miracles are accomplished through the power of faith, and faith requires a commitment to risk. Risk means stepping out, acting on the nudging of the Spirit, even when we're not yet able to see the end results.

As Peter discovered in the boat that day, it's hard to exercise faith while avoiding all possibility for discomfort. A few steps into the water, he began to falter and sink. But Jesus reached out and hoisted him back up. If Peter had been unwilling to risk, think of what he would have missed out on! He had acquired bragging rights as the only documented water-walker in history besides Jesus. Two millenia later, we are still reading about Peter's act of faith as a source for inspiration.

FAILING FORWARD

Risking forward also means not letting the fear of failure hold us back. We all fall down; failure is part of the path to success.

Peter is just one of the heroes in the Bible who failed before or even during their success on other fronts. Genesis 12—the same chapter in which Abraham (then called Abram) in faith left his familiar home at age seventy-five based on God's directive— shows Abraham turning around and in essence prostituting his wife to the Egyptian pharaoh in an act of self-interest and self-preservation. Moses disobeyed God by striking a rock out of anger to draw forth water instead of commanding it by voice as directed, and as a result he was not allowed to enter the Promised Land at the close of a forty-year journey. Samson broke his Nazirite vows to God and lost his anointing until just before his death. David was an adulterer who ordered an assassination on an innocent man, and Paul persecuted early Christians. The list goes on.

We don't lack for contemporary examples as well. Walt Disney lost an early position as a newspaper editor because his employer felt he lacked imagination and good ideas. Oprah was fired from an early job on television. J. K. Rowling was a single mother on public assistance while she went to school and attempted to publish a book. Steven Spielberg was rejected from film school three times. Steven King's novel *Carrie* received thirty rejections before it was published.[1] Basketball great Michael Jordan was demoted from varsity to junior varsity at one point during his high school career.[2] And yet each of these folks went on to make history, "struck down, but not destroyed" (2 Corinthians 4:9 NRSV).

Let's return to Peter and take a look at what happened right before he began to panic. "But when he saw the wind, he was afraid and, beginning to sink, cried out, 'Lord, save me!'"

83

(Matthew 14:30). Peter had become distracted; he had lost his focus on Jesus and instead was focused on the circumstances surrounding him.

We too can become easily distracted, and those distractions can hit us in the form of failed relationships, rejection by those we love and who we believe love us, difficult transitions in life, and a whole host of setbacks. Perhaps the most significant distraction is the belief that being a Christian, a Jesus follower, protects us from challenges. Not so. Jesus declared in John 16:33, "In this world you will have trouble." Oswald Chambers noted in the classic book *My Utmost for His Highest*, "God does not give us overcoming life: He gives us life as we overcome. The strain is the strength. If there is no strain, there is no strength."[3] God will not protect us from challenge, but God does promise to be with us through challenge.

Even in failure, Peter got something else right. He didn't look back to the safety of the boat for his salvation. There was no "Hey guys, throw me a life preserver." He didn't declare, "I've tried this water walking thing, and I'm done with it. I'm going back to the boat." Instead, Peter cried out "Lord, save me!" and continued to trust forward.

PRAYING FORWARD

We risk forward. We fail forward. And in the final action of faith, we pray forward.

We will touch more on prayer in chapter 5, but for now it's important to note the strong bond between the power of faith and the power of prayer. Through prayer, along with time studying God's Word, we encounter the presence of the Holy Spirit, God within us.

Prayer is how we hear and respond to God's leading. When our lives are not working out as we had planned or hoped, we often fall into the trap of climbing on the "trying harder" treadmill. If we don't take time to hear the voice of God, we will lack the courage to follow Jesus. It's hard to get moving, but, like Peter, we can start by taking the first step. We'll be tempted to stay in the risk-free zone, the comfortable place of our present circumstance. But when we do so, we may miss the miracle!

We must be able to pray, "I don't understand it. It seems like darkness is prevailing. But I'm going to trust God and give myself fully to God's outcome."

IN THE STORM

For many of us, it's hard to imagine risking forward, because the storms in our lives are simply too scary or overwhelming. I get it. The waters are rough. In seasons like these, another storm faced by the disciples on the Sea of Galilee comes to mind.

On that occasion, Jesus directed his disciples to cross to the other side of the lake. Jesus climbed on board and settled in for a nap as the crew set sail. But the Sea of Galilee is a shallow freshwater lake in the middle of Israel, and storms can blow in quickly. Soon "a squall came down on the lake, so that the boat was being swamped, and they were in great danger" (Luke 8:23).

This scene is a great analogy for life. We can seem to be sailing along just fine, when conditions suddenly go from calm to chaos. This particular storm must have been a big one. After all, some of the disciples were seasoned fishermen who had spent half their lives on the water. And yet we go on to read in Luke 8:24-25 that the disciples awakened Jesus in great fear, saying, "Master, Master, we're going to drown!"

Jesus, getting up from his nap, "rebuked the wind and the raging waters; the storm subsided, and all was calm." Jesus then asked his disciples the perfect question: "Where is your faith?" The story continues: "In fear and amazement they asked one another, 'Who is this? He commands even the winds and the water, and they obey him.'"

In the midst of life's storms and uncertainties, we cease seeing the potential for God's miracles and instead focus on worry. Jesus naps during the storm while the rest of us experience sleepless nights. As the disciples eventually realized and as Jesus knew all along, we are not in control; God is. Stormy circumstances will not change God's purpose or plans. As Proverbs 19:21 affirms, "Many are the plans in a person's heart, but it is the LORD's purpose that prevails."

Faith is forged in the fiery furnace. Many of us believe in God but don't believe God—that is, we don't trust God. God is going to allow storms in our lives. Why? Because God cares more about shaping our character, our miracle-making potential, than about our comfort. God is more concerned about our salvation than about our sleep.

The disciples reacted to the storm out of fear, but Jesus got up from his nap and rebuked it. Fear is an emotional response; it's not rational. When we feel it rising within us, we must learn to rebuke it, as Jesus did. We need to stop being reactive, to stop staring at the storm and start gazing at the One who is in the boat with us. When we allow fear to influence our decisions, we inhibit God's purposes and God's miracles in our lives.

About a decade ago I purchased a Harley motorcycle, after years of dreaming about it and saving for it so that I could pay cash—a precondition I had agreed to with Carolyn. (A few years later I sold the Harley when my favorite pastime changed from riding to grandparenting—a safer choice but still full of adventure.) As a motorcyclist, I was keenly aware of the inherent risk in riding a bike and never took it for granted. I made sure to complete a great driver's training program, and I kept up my reading about the skills and techniques that I hoped would keep me out of harm's way. One of those techniques was the panic stop. I always found the name a bit of a misnomer, in that to execute a successful panic stop, you have to remain calm and not overreact.

Fortunately I only had to execute the maneuver once. I had been visiting my parents in Lebanon, Ohio, and was going through an intersection, about to turn right. A driver coming from the opposite direction didn't see me and began to veer directly toward my bike. I was able to complete the stop so the car missed me, but it was close. Too close. While trying to avoid a collision, my temptation was to focus on the very hazard I was trying to avoid—in this case, the car—but the truth was that the bike would tend toward the very place where I decided to focus my attention.

In times of crisis, we must confront our psychological tendency to gaze at what we want to avoid, not where we want to go. We believe in Jesus, but we don't stay focused on Jesus. Instead we focus on our own resourcefulness to get us out of the mess, placing our security in our jobs or bank accounts. Sometimes we almost worship our worry, in spite of what Jesus said: "Can any one of you by worrying add a single hour to your life?" (Matthew 6:27). Many of us have invited Jesus into our boats, but we treat him like a life preserver and not the captain.

If there's anyone who knows about storms in our lives and the power of faith for bringing about miracles, it's the members of our Next Step Recovery worshiping community at Ginghamsburg. These are people who know and own fully what it means to be broken. They are also living testimonies to the power of faith in God's grace. The favorite prayer of the recovery community, both at Ginghamsburg and beyond, has always been the Serenity Prayer.

It seems like a great way to wrap up our chapter on the power of activating faith.

> God grant me the serenity
> To accept the things I cannot change;
> Courage to change the things I can;
> And wisdom to know the difference.
>
> Living one day at a time;
> Enjoying one moment at a time;
> Accepting hardships as the pathway to peace;
> Taking, as He did, this sinful world
> As it is, not as I would have it;
> Trusting that He will make all things right
> If I surrender to His Will;
> So that I may be reasonably happy in this life
> And supremely happy with Him
> Forever in the next.
> (prayer attributed to Reinhold Niebuhr, 1892–1971)

REFLECTION

How will you activate your faith in your journey with Jesus?

- Name an area or circumstance within your life where you are struggling with doubt. In what ways are you doubting God's ability or willingness to bring about change or progress? Confess to God your doubt and pray, "Lord, I believe; help my unbelief."

- Have you developed a life mission statement that guides you in activating faith? You may want to look at my book *Dare to Dream: Creating a God-sized Mission Statement for Your Life.*

- In what parts of your life are you sitting back and waiting for God to bring about a miracle? Do you have debt issues? Do you need a job or a new job? Do you have a relationship that is badly in need of repair? Name one proactive step you will take this week to add your initiative to God's divine intervention.

- Is risk aversion holding you back from taking the next step into God's preferred future for your life? Think of a risk you should take, identify the worst possible outcome, and ask yourself, "Can I survive this worst-case scenario?" If the answer is yes, start risking. As the apostle Paul said, "I can do all this through him who gives me strength" (Philippians 4:13).

5

ACTIVATE THE POWER OF PRAYER

5

ACTIVATE THE POWER
OF PRAYER

*One of those days Jesus went out to a mountainside to
pray, and spent the night praying to God.*

(Luke 6:12)

A few years ago at Ginghamsburg, we informally surveyed our
church family to determine which spiritual discipline they felt was
most important to their faith journey, as well as which discipline
they struggled the most to practice. In both cases, prayer seemed
to be either number one or number two on the list.

Prayer is also the discipline I admittedly can struggle with the
most. As a busy pastor who also wrestles with attention deficit
disorder, I find that it's all too easy to neglect prayer in my rush

to meet and complete the urgencies of each day. Yet, I know that prayer is foundational to my relationship with God and was also Jesus' most practiced discipline.

JESUS AND PRAYER

The Gospels—the four short books describing Jesus' mission and ministry on planet earth—reference Jesus praying more than sixty times. Jesus, who "made himself nothing by taking the very nature of a servant, being made in human likeness" (Philippians 2:7), knew that prayer was key to the power exercised in and through his life.

After healing the invalid at the Pool of Bethesda, Jesus was accused by the Jewish leaders of breaking the Sabbath. Jesus defended himself, saying, "Very truly I tell you, the Son can do nothing by himself; he can do only what he sees his Father doing, because whatever the Father does the Son also does" (John 5:19). Jesus reiterated this belief a few moments later when he said, "By myself I can do nothing" (v. 30). Jesus further proclaimed his reliance on God's power, accessible through prayer, in John 8:28: "So Jesus said, 'When you have lifted up the Son of Man, then you will know that I am he and that I do nothing on my own but speak just what the Father has taught me.'"

This is why we find Jesus praying at crucial moments in his ministry. Jesus spent the night in solitude and prayer before selecting the small group of followers who would be most key in founding the church: "One of those days Jesus went out to a mountainside to pray, and spent the night praying to God. When morning came, he called his disciples to him and chose twelve of them, whom he also designated apostles" (Luke 6:12-13). Prayer also preceded Jesus' most remarkable miracles. In John 11:41-43, when Lazarus had been dead for four days, Jesus prayed before calling out to Lazarus to exit the tomb. This same power of prayer demonstrated by Jesus is essential to the miracles that God will do in and through our own lives.

FOUR ESSENTIAL DYNAMICS

In the pages ahead, we will explore four essential dynamics of prayer: wait, obey, expect, and act. I know of no better example of these four dynamics at work than Joshua 3:1-8 in the Old Testament, Scripture with which Jesus would have been quite familiar.

After escaping slavery in Egypt under Moses's leadership, the original generation of former Hebrew slaves was forced to wander in the desert for forty years. This occurred because of the Israelites' repeated acts of disobedience toward God's directives and their constant grumbling about God's provision, accompanied by occasional bouts of longing to return to their "safe" bonds back in Egypt. In Joshua 3, the new generation, led by Moses's successor Joshua, was ready to enter God's Promised Land. Yet even then, after forty years, there were barriers to cross and enemies to battle. After all, the forces of resistance always stand between the people of God and their inheritance. The people's first challenge would be to cross the Jordan River during harvest season, while the river was at flood stage.

The people would not cross the Jordan alone; the ark of the covenant would precede them. Joshua instructed the officers to tell them,

> "When you see the ark of the covenant of the LORD
> your God, and the Levitical priests carrying it, you are
> to move out from your positions and follow it. Then you

will know which way to go, since you have never been
this way before."

(Joshua 3:3-4)

The ark carried the stone tablets that had been inscribed by God's own hand with the Ten Commandments, and the Israelites believed that the ark represented the active presence of God in their midst. So holy and powerful were the ark's contents that even the priests and Levites who carried the ark could not see it directly; as it traveled, it was always hidden under a veil of skins and cloth.

The Jordan River was not an exception to the "ark first" strategy; the ark and its carriers always led the way whenever the people broke camp and traveled to their next God-directed place. Each time before the ark was moved, the people offered the prayer that Moses had initiated in Numbers 10:35:

> *"Rise up, Lord!*
> *May your enemies be scattered;*
> *may your foes flee before you."*

Given the sacredness of what the ark represented, the people were required to keep their distance. In fact, Joshua directed the people to keep a distance of about two thousand cubits between themselves and the ark, or the length of seven to eight football fields including both end zones!

Wait

When we want to make our next move to find God's miracle in or through our own lives, we too, like the Hebrew people, need to place a holy space between our seeking and our action. In the busyness and distractions of daily life, it's easy to miss the most important voice. We would rather move quickly to pursue our own "good" rather than wait to attain God's great. It's critical that we learn to wait in prayer, not moving ahead of God's directive.

Waiting in prayer is not a time of speaking but of listening. It's not the moment for praying "help me," "heal me," or "hear me." Instead, as Psalm 46:10 directs us, we are to "be still, and know that I am God." When we fail to make this holy space, when we jump to action, our prayer life is likely to devolve into praying, "Lord, save me from the messes of my own making."

As a person who is quick to move, I sometimes have to remind myself just to breathe as I await God's next plan for my life or the lives of those I care about. In fact, as pointed out by Franciscan friar Richard Rohr, the word *Yahweh*, the unspeakable name for God in Hebrew, is an "attempt to replicate and imitate the very sound of inhalation and exhalation." In other words, in the very act of breathing to sustain life we are speaking the name of God. Rohr writes, "This makes God our first and last word as we enter and leave the world."[1] As the lyrics to popular Hillsong praise music proclaims, "This is the air I breathe, your holy presence living in me."[2] I find that breathing in and out the name of God helps me to wait in prayer and remember that "in him we live and move and have our being" (Acts 17:28). As Jesus declared, "I am the vine; you are the branches. If you remain in me and I in you, you will bear much fruit; apart from me you can do nothing" (John 15:5). Frankly, we *should* do nothing unless first we have waited for God in prayer. God is not only with me; God is in me. The holy space of waiting reminds me, as it did King Jehoshaphat, that "the battle is not yours, but God's" (2 Chronicles 20:15). This day and the battle belong to the Lord.

We don't want to get ahead of God. Like the Israelites and the ark, we want to be sure that the Spirit of God goes before us. We can't win the battle—force the miracle—by relying on our own strength: "'Not by might nor by power, but by my Spirit,' says the LORD Almighty" (Zechariah 4:6).

The New Testament also shows the power of waiting in prayer. In the Book of Acts, just before Jesus was taken into heaven, he commanded his disciples,

> *"Do not leave Jerusalem, but wait for the gift my Father promised, which you have heard me speak about. For John baptized with water, but in a few days you will be baptized with the Holy Spirit."*
>
> *(Acts 1:4-5)*

The followers spent the next ten days praying together in one place up to the day of Pentecost. They trusted Jesus enough to wait for the gift that the Father had already promised.

I'm not sure I would have been as patient in waiting as those early, committed followers. My temptation is always to get ahead of God, both creating and then living under the illusion that I can control whatever situation or circumstance I am confronting. As a pastor, dad, and grandfather, I like those in my care also to believe that I am confident and capable at all times and in all circumstances.

Two years ago in late January, my family and I were busily preparing for a long-planned cruise that would depart from Fort Lauderdale, Florida, and then make its way to the Bahamas, St. Thomas, and St. Maarten. Carolyn and I, our children, their spouses, and all our grandkids were to sail the seas together. Normally such a trip would have been unaffordable, but I had been able to arrange this once-in-a-lifetime opportunity as part of my retainer for serving as one of the educational cruise's speakers. Plans for the cruise had been fourteen months in the making. As you might imagine, the grandchildren in particular were excited. For months their moms and dads had been promising this exotic vacation and a great time with their cousins, aunts and uncles, and Papa and Nana.

At the time my son, Jonathan; his wife, Stacy; and their two (now three) children lived in Philadelphia, a city that was predicted to be hit by a huge blizzard on the same day their flight was scheduled to leave for the start of our vacation. Jonathan, an orthopedic surgeon, called me a few days before, asking what he should do. Should he reschedule his pending surgery patients with other surgeons, not a great option, and have the family catch an earlier flight? Jonathan knew that his kids, and all of us, would be deeply disappointed if this long-anticipated vacation plan were ruined.

It was one time when I managed to practice what I preach. I said, "Jonathan, let me pray about this." For the next twenty-four hours I stopped, waited, and listened—not my typical MO. A day later I called Jonathan back and said, "This is what I am hearing from God. We are to wait, be still, and see what God will do." Jon stayed in Philadelphia to perform his surgeries, and he and the family left Philly on Friday afternoon, on one of the last flights safely out of the soon-to-be-closed airport.

It was just a cruise, a family vacation, and not a matter of life or death. But God delivered on the promised gift. I don't understand it; I was just glad to accept it. May I always do the same when the stakes are high and a miracle is needed. For forty years Moses prayed every time before the ark was moved, "Rise up, LORD! May your enemies be scattered; may your foes flee before you" (Numbers 10:35). Don't get ahead of God.

Obey

Joshua's first instruction to the Hebrew people had been to wait, by following behind the ark and the presence of God that it represented. In Joshua 3:5, he gave his second directive to the people as they prepared to cross the Jordan: "Consecrate yourselves, for tomorrow the Lord will do amazing things among you." Joshua was telling the Israelites to sanctify themselves, giving themselves completely over to God's will before they took the first step toward realizing God's miracle. In other words, they were to obey.

Consecrate means to be set apart wholly to God for God's purposes. If there is anything I have learned in my nearly five decades of following Jesus, it's that God won't bless disobedience, but God certainly will honor obedience. The psalmist put it this way:

> For the Lord God is a sun and shield;
>   the Lord bestows favor and honor;
> no good thing does he withhold
>   from those whose walk is blameless.
>   (Psalm 84:11)

In the twentieth- and twenty-first-century church, we have developed some mistaken ideas about prayer, paying less attention to the priority of obedience. We rely on easy "believism" instead of following Jesus in the way of the cross, and we toss out prayers of convenience instead of understanding the priority of obedience in alignment with God's will. Jesus indicated in John 14:13, "I will do whatever you ask in my name." This does not just mean tacking "in Jesus' name" on to the end of each prayer; in fact, when we use that phrase without yielding fully to Christ's authority, it's a violation of the fourth commandment: "Thou shalt not take the name of the Lord thy God in vain" (Exodus 20:7 KJV).

When we dare to pray in Jesus' name for a miracle, we had best be submitting ourselves fully to God's will. In essence, we are praying "I pledge my obedience, I pledge my allegiance, I pledge my life." Not my will but yours be done. John Wesley's covenant prayer still gives me chills each time I read it.

> I am no longer my own, but yours.
> Put me to what thou will, rank me with whom you will....
> I freely and heartily yield all things to your pleasure and
>   disposal.
> And now, O glorious and blessed God, Father, Son and
>   Holy Spirit,
> You are mine, and I am yours.
> So be it.... Amen

(Methodist Worship Book, p. 290)

We are to consecrate ourselves, committing to obedience, before we ever know what God's answer to our prayer may be.

Expect

When Joshua directed the Israelites to consecrate themselves, he added "for tomorrow the LORD will do amazing things among you" (Joshua 3:5). Expectation determines outcome.

When I arrived at Ginghamsburg Church in 1979, it was a semirural congregation of fewer than ninety people with a $27,000 annual budget. Today, it is a thriving multi-campus movement of over four thousand. Sometimes people ask me, "Are you surprised that this happened, especially here in this unlikely place?" Honestly, I have to answer no. I expected it.

One chilly spring day shortly after my arrival, I spent the day alone in a field behind the church seeking God's face, asking for the vision of what God wanted to do through this place. God obliged! Today I am delighted but not surprised. I also can't take credit. I sum it up to folks by saying, "I am simply the donkey that God rode in on." I also still believe that greater things yet will happen in this place.

In Mark 6, Jesus had returned to his hometown of Nazareth to boldly proclaim the gospel, fresh off of accolades elsewhere in Galilee. Yet his former neighbors were simply aghast. Who did Jesus, this carpenter's son, think he was? They asked each other,

> *"Isn't this Mary's son and the brother of James, Joseph, Judas and Simon? Aren't his sisters here with us?"*
> *And they took offense at him. . . . He could not do any*
> *miracles there, except lay his hands on a few sick people*
> *and heal them. He was amazed at their lack of faith.*
> (*Mark 6:3, 5-6*)

Their low expectations determined their minimal outcomes. What a missed opportunity!

Jesus, by contrast, directed us to pray with great expectation: "Therefore I tell you, whatever you ask for in prayer, believe that you have received it, and it will be yours" (Mark 11:24). How easy it can be to forget that Jesus is the fulfillment of God's promises: "For no matter how many promises God has made, they are 'Yes' in Christ. And so through him the 'Amen' is spoken by us to the glory of God" (2 Corinthians 1:20).

My life experience has proven to me repeatedly that where God gives vision, he also gives provision. My time in that Ohio field is but one example. But there are still occasions when I have to watch the downsized, misplaced, or disappointing expectations that come into my head. Perhaps it's one reason that when I have a serious matter for prayer, I sometimes take it to the small, original chapel that thirty-nine years ago was the only Ginghamsburg Church. I find it easier to pray with faith and expectation when I'm in a place where I've already witnessed God perform a miracle.

The Old Testament prophet Elijah is a great example of the miracles that happen when we pray with expectation and trust.

In First Kings 17, Elijah told the evil king Ahab that a drought would overtake the land for the next few years as a result of the royal couple's allegiance to the god of Baal. True enough, the drought started as promised and lingered. In the third year Elijah, having made God's point, returned to Ahab and wound up in an unfair matchup between Elijah's God and the false prophets of Baal. Unfair, of course, meaning that there was no possibility of the living God losing that bout. Once Elijah through God's power had demonstrated Baal's complete inefficacy, he felt confident that ending the drought would be clearly understood by all witnesses as a demonstration of God's power, not Baal's.

Before Elijah even prayed for God to send rain, he was completely expectant that God would deliver the miracle, and so he told Ahab, "Go, eat and drink, for there is the sound of a heavy rain" (1 Kings 18:41). Elijah then proceeded to pray. Rain did not begin immediately, but Elijah persevered, and ultimately a little cloud rose up from the sea, "as small as a man's hand" (v. 44). Still not discouraged, Elijah kept praying, and a short time later "the sky grew black with clouds, the wind rose, a heavy rain started falling" (v. 45). Elijah knew what it meant to pray with perfect expectation.

We see this same confident expectation when Nehemiah, after fasting and waiting in prayer for several days, asked God to provide for a seemingly impossible and dangerous mission to rebuild the destroyed wall surrounding a crippled Jerusalem. We see it in Daniel when he ignored the royal decree to pray only to the king of the land and instead continued his regular discipline of praying to the one true God three times daily, in spite of being taken to the lions' den. In both cases, God answered their prayers.

My daughter-in-law, Stacy, has always done a great job of helping Carolyn and me be engaged, long-distance grandparents, frequently sending us pictures and videos of our young granddaughter and grandson. During the time when we were planning the family cruise I described earlier, Stacy texted us a drawing by my granddaughter Addison that still holds a special place in my memory. It was a fine drawing for a five-year-old, but what made it so memorable was what Stacy had written reassuringly at the top for her daughter—and really for Carolyn and me as we anxiously awaited the next grim weather report: "Now faith is confidence in what we hope for and assurance about what we do not see" (Hebrews 11:1). Amen. Our faith in God's answers should never be dictated by circumstances, but by God's promises.

Too often we stop praying because we don't see any tangible difference that prayer has made. We become impatient for a miracle. We allow circumstances to get between God and us, instead of putting God between us and our circumstances. Pray and be expectant, standing on the promises of God.

Act

Let's return to the story of Joshua.

> And the LORD said to Joshua, "Today I will begin to exalt you in the eyes of all Israel, so they may know that I am with you as I was with Moses. Tell the priests who carry the ark of the covenant: 'When you reach the edge of the Jordan's waters, go and stand in the river.'"
>
> (Joshua 3:7-8)

Simple enough, right? All the priests had to do was to enter the river to usher in God's miracle. But, no! We read a few verses later, "Now the Jordan is at flood stage all during harvest" (Joshua 3:15).

Have you ever seen a rapidly flowing river at flood stage? The thought of stepping into the strong, churning current would be intimidating at best and life-threatening at worst. Why does it seem that God always asks us to do something that is hard? Why couldn't the Israelites have reached the Jordan during a drought?

The difficult circumstances in which God may direct us to act often produce immediate doubt. But it's only when the Jordan Rivers in our lives are at flood stage that God's supernatural miracle is both possible—and evident. At "flood stage" we clearly can't claim the credit for success, because the solution seems impossible. In normal circumstances it's not a miracle, because the solution is easy.

If you are like me, you tend to first see and then believe. But, where is the faith in that? God's miraculous intervention in and through our lives happens when we first believe, and then receive. Remember, a miracle has two components: divine intervention and human initiative.

Naaman, commander of a powerful king's army, would never see his leprosy miraculously healed until he humbled himself, trusted in God's directive through the prophet Elisha, and washed himself in that same Jordan River (2 Kings 5). Likewise, the poor widow would have been forced to turn over her two sons for slavery if she had not followed Elisha's instructions, gathering as many jars from her neighbors as possible so her small amount of oil could be miraculously multiplied and sold to support her family and settle her debts (2 Kings 4:1-7).

In the story of Joshua, the River Jordan would not stop its rushing flow until the priests did their part, trusting in God's promise to Joshua. "Yet as soon as the priests who carried the ark reached the Jordan and their feet touched the water's edge, the water from upstream stopped flowing" (Joshua 3:15-16). Note that the miracle was triggered when the priests touched the water.

How often do we let fear, doubt, or simply disobedience derail us from experiencing God's miracle? Instead, we are to risk out in faith, step into the rushing water, be willing to get our feet wet. Right now, this day, where are you failing to act in faith?

Karen Perry Smith serves at times as my writing partner. Karen left a well-paying corporate position in 2002, took a 40 percent pay cut, and joined the Ginghamsburg staff team. On the surface this was not a wise decision for the primary breadwinner of a family, and Karen almost backed out. She shared with me once that as she prayed and read the Word, seeking God's direction on this major decision, the following scripture stopped her in her tracks, and has served as a life verse ever since: "Taste and see that the LORD is good" (Psalm 34:8). Taste and then *see*. Believe and then *receive*. Karen, a careful risk manager in both her professional and personal life, had wanted it to work the other way around. If we are going to seek God's directive in prayer for miracles in and through our lives, then we had better be prepared to act on what we hear! It's not a wait and see; it's an act and see.

One of the saints in the church during my early days at Ginghamsburg was Gertie. Gertie was much beloved within the congregation, a kind and generous woman who radiated warmth. As we became acquainted, I asked Gertie about her family. When I saw her at church, she was always alone. She shared with me that she had been married to her husband, Denver, for sixty years, but that Denver was not much of a churchgoer. I asked if I could stop by sometime and meet Denver, and she agreed, somewhat reluctantly, implying kindly that Denver did not have much use for churches, or pastors for that matter. I had a great visit with Denver. He was warm, friendly, and enjoyed showing me around his home and talking about his pastimes and pursuits. I invited him to join Gertie in worship with us sometime.

As it turned out, a few weeks later I looked out into the congregation and there sat Denver right next to Gertie. A few weeks after that he chose to be baptized, and Denver became a strong Jesus follower, tither, and servant. I knew that for sixty years Gertie had been praying for Denver to know Jesus. Curious, I finally asked Denver why he had never come to church with Gertie before. He replied, "She never asked. You did."

The fourth dynamic of praying for miracles is to do what God is telling you to do. As Jesus said, "Blessed rather are those who hear the word of God and obey it" (Luke 11:28).

Where are you seeking a miracle in your life? Finances, relationships, improved health? Listen to the apostle Paul: "I tell you, now is the time of God's favor, now is the day of salvation (2 Corinthians 6:2).

It's time to act on what you have heard God say.

Day-to-Day Miracles

Prayer is not just something to pull out from our Christian toolbox and brandish when urgent miracles are needed. The seed for show-stopping miracles begins in praying for and appreciating the humbler miracles each day, remembering our daily dependence on God.

This is why, as the Israelites wandered in the wilderness for forty years, the miracle of the manna occurred each day. "Then the LORD said to Moses, 'I will rain down bread from heaven for you. The people are to go out each day and gather enough for that day'" (Exodus 16:4). The people needed to be reminded of their daily dependence on God's provision, not enabled to stockpile accumulated stores that would allow them more easily to forget "from whence cometh my help" (Psalm 121:1 KJV). This is also

107

why Jesus reminded his disciples to pray, "Give us today our daily bread" (Matthew 6:11). Perhaps God doesn't trust us with major miracles until we understand our reliance on the small ones.

Ann Voskamp's book *One Thousand Gifts* emphasizes the role that gratitude plays in realizing and recognizing miracles in our daily lives, repeatedly noting that "*eucharisteo* [giving of thanks] always precedes the miracle."[3] The giving of thanks for what God has done and continues to do daily in and through our lives provides fertile ground for future miracles. The psalmist assures us,

> "The one who offers thanksgiving as his sacrifice
> glorifies me;
>> to one who orders his way rightly
>> I will show the salvation of God!"
>
> (Psalm 50:23 ESV)

We see day-to-day miracles in practice from Jesus as he prepares to feed five thousand households with five loaves and two fish. "Taking the five loaves and the two fish and looking up to heaven, he gave thanks and broke them. Then he gave them to the disciples to distribute to the people" (Luke 9:16). Before calling Lazarus from the tomb, "Jesus looked up and said, 'Father, I thank you that you have heard me. I knew that you always hear me, but I said this for the benefit of the people standing here, that they may believe that you sent me'" (John 11:41-42).

The apostle Paul counsels the Ephesians, "Sing and make music from your heart to the Lord, always giving thanks to God the Father for everything, in the name of our Lord Jesus Christ" (Ephesians 5:19-20). Gratitude, the giving of thanks, is not optional. We certainly are to thank God for the big miracles, but also for the small ones. As Paul implied in his letter to the

Ephesians and declares outright in 1 Thessalonians 5:18, we are to "give thanks in all circumstances; for this is God's will for you in Christ Jesus."

Some of those circumstances may include times when we don't receive the specific miracle for which we have been praying. Faith means trusting God even when the answer appears to be no. It means trusting God's heart when we can't see God's hand, being assured of "how much more will your Father in heaven give good gifts to those who ask him!" (Matthew 7:9-11).

When I think about God seeming to say no, I find it instructive to consider my own parenting experience. When we love our kids, we like them to be happy. It's easier to say yes and be rewarded with smiles than to say no and be met with grumbles and gripes. It took energy and perseverance on my part to say no and watch my popularity rating plummet even lower than it already was with a thirteen-year-old daughter; it would have been easier if I had chosen the path of least resistance, acceding to every wish and whim no matter how impractical. Yet, as a responsible parent, I knew it was my job to sacrifice the easy for the important if I really loved my kids.

God always answers prayer, but God may not honor our self-selected strategy. God is not a vending machine with prayer as our required payment for plopping out that bag of kettle-cooked salt-and-vinegar chips we've been craving. But this same Father will be only too happy to provide us this day our daily bread.

Seeing God in the day-to-day will make it easier to trust God in a crisis. Jesus reminds us, "Do not worry about your life, what you will eat; or about your body, what you will wear.... Do not be afraid, little flock, for your Father has been pleased to give you the kingdom" (Luke 12:22, 32).

Praying God's Miracles
into the World

Jesus pronounced his mission statement, which he shared while reading from the Book of Isaiah in the synagogue:

"The Spirit of the Lord is on me,
  because he has anointed me
  to proclaim good news to the poor.
He has sent me to proclaim freedom for the prisoners
  and recovery of sight for the blind,
to set the oppressed free,
  to proclaim the year of the Lord's favor."
                                        (Luke 4:18-19)

In the original, Isaiah goes on to prophesy that those restored will "rebuild the ancient ruins and restore the places long devastated" (Isaiah 61:4).

In these scriptures, God is not only inviting us to wait expectantly in prayer, to obey, and to act in anticipation of miracles in our own lives and the lives of those around us; God also wants us to be part of his "kingdom of God" mission to all of planet earth—to be part of God's rescue team. How are we to identify and engage in the larger miracles that God wants to do for the world that God so loves? The bottom line is that God plans to accomplish his miracles through us.

Jesus said, "You did not choose me, but I chose you and appointed you so that you might go and bear fruit—fruit that will last—and so that whatever you ask in my name the Father will give you" (John 15:16).

Nehemiah gives us a great example of how prayer precedes progress when it comes to miracles of restoration. Nehemiah, as mentioned earlier in this chapter, initiated a mission to restore the wall around Jerusalem, a project that held economic, political, and spiritual implications for the Jewish people living in captivity. Talk about a place long devastated! The walls had been destroyed by Nebuchadnezzar more than a century before. Plus, the physical and logistical task itself would be no small feat. The year was roughly 445 BC, almost 2,400 years before the invention of the backhoe!

Nehemiah's first action was to sit down. He understood the importance of waiting in prayer and pausing to assess, take inventory, and face the reality and magnitude of the job at hand. After assessing the situation, Nehemiah wept. In our comfortable lives and our familiar pews, it's easy to ignore the world's pain. Perhaps we should cry more. God uses people to bring about miracles when their hearts break for the same things that break God's heart.

We then read, "For some days I mourned" (Nehemiah 1:4). Nehemiah was experiencing what it's like to help carry God's pain for the least and the lost. In addition to mourning, verse 4 tells us that Nehemiah "fasted and prayed." The fasting reminded Nehemiah that he was hungry for something greater. He had reached a point of utter dissatisfaction with the comfortable complacency in which he had been living. In prayer, he then made himself available for God's greater purpose. Sound familiar? We can draw a number of comparisons with Jesus' urgent time of prayer and surrender in the Garden of Gethsemane for God's greater purpose.

Nehemiah began his prayer in verse 5, first acknowledging God's greatness: "LORD, the God of heaven, the great and awesome God…" Nehemiah knew that a prerequisite for a miracle is embracing God as ultimate authority and creator, greater than any obstacle or resistant force, deserving of all respect. Trusting forward for the miraculous is almost impossible when we make our God of unlimited power and resources too small for the opportunity at hand.

Nehemiah continued his prayer in verse 5 by recognizing God as the One "who keeps his covenant of love with those who love him and keep his commandments." As God had earlier reassured Abraham, "I will establish my covenant as an everlasting covenant between me and you and your descendants after you for the generations to come, to be your God and the God of your descendants after you" (Genesis 17:7). This covenant was an unbreakable promise, an unshakeable agreement, about which the apostle Paul later proclaimed, "God's gifts and his call are irrevocable" (Romans 11:29).

In verse 6, Nehemiah rightly identified his role in God's kingdom as "servant," one who works at the will and call of the master, not a volunteer who deigns to stack a few stones on top of the wall according to his own packed and self-prioritized schedule.

Nehemiah then confessed the sins of his heart, his house, and his country. Coming clean, being honest, trusting God with our stuff—and we all have stuff—is a potent part of any prayer life, especially when we are in the miracle business. Such heart integrity allows us to align our thoughts, motives, actions, and lifestyles with our stated beliefs and commitments. Confession means declaring we will not rationalize or compromise. It's more than saying, "I'm sorry." It's repenting, literally turning and going the other way.

Nehemiah next prayed, "LORD, let your ear be attentive to the prayer of this your servant and to the prayer of your servants who delight in revering your name" (v. 11). In essence Nehemiah was praying, "Are you in this, God? Is this a God thing or just a good thing?" In asking this, Nehemiah recognized that the outcome ultimately depended upon God. Nehemiah would not move out in front of the ark of the covenant, so to speak. As Moses before him had said to the Lord, "If your presence will not go with me, do not bring us up from here" (Exodus 33:15 ESV).

Have you confirmed that that for which you've been praying is where God is moving? Have you asked God, "Is this where I am supposed to be?" Remember, miracles have two components: divine intervention and human initiative. The latter alone will never result in a successful miracle-making endeavor. We can't do it by ourselves, no matter how good our intentions or committed our hearts are toward the desired outcome.

Nehemiah ended his prayer with commitment: "Give your servant success today by granting him favor in the presence of this man" (v. 11). Immediately afterward, Nehemiah followed his prayer with action, requesting permission from the pagan king he served to leave his post and work on restoring the wall. By acting, Nehemiah demonstrated that prayer is not an end in itself; it is a prelude to action, the opening door to a miracle.

Where on earth is God inviting you to be part of God's restorative purpose? Where can you be God's coworker in bringing about extraordinary miracles that will redeem the lost and set the oppressed free? Both everyday miracles and miracles of biblical proportion are possible when we activate the power of prayer in our lives.

REFLECTION

How will you transform your prayer life in your journey with Jesus?

- Name an important decision that you believe you will be required to make within the next three to six months. How will you prioritize prayer to seek God's best instead of your own best?

- Where might low expectations be holding you back from experiencing God's miracle? Which promise of God do you need to remember is a yes in Christ Jesus?

- Are you struggling to experience the power and promise of God in your prayer life? Where have you witnessed God's miracles in the past, so that you can revisit that place for a time of focused prayer and listening for God?

- Name three or four "day-to-day" miracles in your life. Upon waking this week, take time to thank God for each miracle.

- What are you observing in the world around you that is tugging at your heart right now? How will you wait, obey, expect, and act to be part of what God wants to do through you?

6
ACTIVATE HEALTH
AND HEALING

6

ACTIVATE HEALTH
AND HEALING

At sunset, the people brought to Jesus all who had various kinds of sickness, and laying his hands on each one, he healed them.

(Luke 4:40)

More than 700 verses of the 3,779 total across the four Gospels deal with some type of physical or mental healing, including resurrection of the dead. And this undoubtedly represents only a fraction of Jesus' healings during his relatively brief ministry on earth.

Clearly, medical science would have been in its infancy during Jesus' lifetime; Hippocrates, who has been called the "father of modern medicine," had not been born until 460 BC. Disease, distress, and short life expectancy would have been the norm. People of Jesus' time were desperate for treatments, decreased suffering—and miracles.

Fast-forward to the twenty-first century. People in the least developed or war-torn countries today still struggle for care and treatment, much as our first-century ancestors did. Even the United States, one of the wealthiest nations in the world with extensive science and treatment options, does not have this health thing completely figured out.

According to the Center for Disease Control (CDC), heart disease, the nation's number-one killer, claims over six hundred thousand US lives annually.[1] One contributor to the high death rate from heart disease is obesity. In the United States, two in three adults are considered to be overweight or obese.[2] We might as well be holding a loaded gun to our head.

And obesity isn't our only method of choice for self-destruction. A recent article in the *New York Times* featured my own backyard, Montgomery County, Ohio, where Dayton is located, detailing a recent month in which the county coroner's office processed 145 cases of opioid overdose. Tragically, the death rate for overdose cases in the counties surrounding Ginghamsburg's campuses has since accelerated. That same article in the *New York Times* reported CDC statistics that ninety-one people in the United States were dying every day from opioid overdose. Help us, Jesus! We need some serious miracles.[3] In the early days of the Israelites' period of slavery in Egypt, God identified himself as Yahweh-Rapha, "the Lord who heals," as translated in this passage:

> *"If you listen carefully to the LORD your God and do*
> *what is right in his eyes, if you pay attention to his*
> *commands and keep all his decrees, I will not bring on*

you any of the diseases I brought on the Egyptians, for I am the Lord, who heals you."

(Exodus 15:26)

Similarly, the Old Testament presents story after story of God's healing work in the world through his prophets and other agents. It's no surprise that restoring people to health—physical, mental, spiritual—was a key component of Jesus' earthly ministry. Healing is even named in Jesus' mission statement: "The Spirit of the Lord is on me, because he has anointed me ... to proclaim freedom for the prisoners and recovery of sight for the blind, to set the oppressed free ... " (Luke 4:18). Yet, as we have emphasized in our study of miracles to this point, healing miracles require divine intervention *plus* human initiative. We are to be active participants in our own healing and in healing the fallen world around us.

One of Jesus' miracles that best demonstrates what this partnership looks like is the healing of the paralytic at the Pool of Bethesda, recounted in John 5. Let's take a closer look at that event, which beautifully illustrates the three components of our part in bringing about miracles of healing: get up, pick up, and walk.

Do You Want to Get Well?

Some time later, Jesus went up to Jerusalem for one of the Jewish festivals. Now there is in Jerusalem near the Sheep Gate a pool, which in Aramaic is called Bethesda and which is surrounded by five covered colonnades. Here a great number of disabled people used to lie—the blind, the lame, the paralyzed.

(John 5:1-3)

The archaeological remains of the Pool of Bethesda, unearthed in the nineteenth century, are located in today's Muslim quarter of Jerusalem. The name Bethesda reportedly means either "house of mercy" or "house of grace." Healing spas and baths were common in the Roman world, and this site was known to be used throughout the first century as an *asclepeion*, or a healing temple dedicated to the Greek god of medicine, Asclepius.

In the passage above, Jesus was about to have a very personal encounter with one of the many disabled folks who were lingering by the pool, hoping to be healed. It's important to note in Scripture, descriptive names for health conditions held deeply spiritual connotations. Often physical dysfunction was code for spiritual illness. Spiritual issues were often at the root of the presenting physical ailment.

John's account of Jesus' visit to the pool quickly narrows in on one man, who had lain in a state of paralysis for thirty-eight years. We can't know for sure, given the many people at the pool, why Jesus may have singled out this particular man. But he likely evoked extra compassion when Jesus learned that the man's condition had lingered almost for a lifetime, given average life expectancy around the start of the first century AD.

When we step back and assess the spiritual implications of Jesus' encounter with this man, we see that first, John names the condition from which the man suffered. Naming what troubles us, naming our places of suffering or brokenness, is always the first step toward transformation. That's why the first of the Twelve Steps for Alcoholic Anonymous is: "We admitted we were powerless over alcohol—that our lives had become unmanageable." If we won't name it, if we don't own it, then we can't heal it.

John describes the man as an invalid, and in verse 7 the King James translation refers to him as impotent, or powerless. When we are convinced of our own powerlessness, we are stuck. We who describe ourselves as Jesus followers are stuck when we claim a form of faith but are not experiencing its power. That's called spiritual impotency.

People who perceive themselves as powerless often begin to see themselves as victims. We begin to make excuses. Tradition held that sometimes the waters at the Pool of Bethesda would bubble, or be stirred, and the first ill person who made it into the pool during this stirring would be healed. This "invalid" of thirty-eight years had his own excuse for inaction: "I have no one to help me into the pool when the water is stirred. While I am trying to get in, someone else goes down ahead of me" (John 5:7). The man had become comfortable in his discomfort, accustomed to his current circumstance, a firm believer in his own excuses. His "day job" had become lying by the pool week after week, year after year, changing nothing, making excuses, eventually expecting nothing. He was stuck.

This man was by no means an aberration of human behavior. We too find all kinds of paralyzing excuses for inaction. I don't have time. I'm too busy. I'm too old. I'm too young. I can't afford it. We allow ourselves to be held back by the fear of disappointment, vulnerability, and potential pain. Like the invalid, we learn to become comfortable in our current state of unhealth. Jesus does not want to leave us there!

All of us, even if thankfully we are not currently confronting a life-or-death illness, have resistant habits or life patterns that keep us from being all that God created us to be. As Christians, we tend to minimize the word *salvation*. We hear the expression "God is in the business of saving souls," and we leave it at that. Well, it's not just about our souls. God is a triune being—Father, Son, and Holy Spirit, three unique persons that are one God. Since we are made

121

in God's image, we too are triune beings—body, mind, and spirit, one distinct person with three parts. God wants to heal all of us, not just our souls. In fact, one definition of *soteria*, the Greek word for salvation, is "health" or "soundness in health." For God, salvation is about wellness for all of us, and for the "whole" of each of us.

In John 5:6, Jesus asked the man a question that I believe all of us desiring a miracle of healing or transformation need to answer for our own places of unhealth: "Do you want to get well?" (John 5:6). Do you really want to get well, or would you rather stay on your same old mat, paralyzed in the same old state? Too many of us choose to linger in and live with the pain of staying the same, resigning ourselves to the status quo, versus courageously taking that first proactive step toward healing and health.

Jesus, ignoring the man's excuses, gave him clear instructions: Get up! Pick up your mat and walk (v. 8). Note that the healing happened through the man's faith actions as he left his mat and followed Jesus' directive. Jesus didn't wave a magic wand before the man attempted to climb to his feet. As we've said before, there's a big difference between magic and a miracle: miracles include both divine intervention *and* human initiative. Seldom is it "Pray" then "Whoosh! I'm healed!" If we want to get well, we too need to get up, pick up, and walk. Let's look at these three steps in more detail.

GET UP

The first thing we need to do to activate healing in our lives, to bring about change, is to *get up*. Getting up is an intentional, physical action. The man in John 5 had been lying in the same state for thirty-eight years. Getting up for most of us may mean doing something that our bodies are not in the habit of doing, or at least doing well.

I have discovered when it comes to my physical health that my body is a good servant but a terrible leader. To accomplish all the things I need to do each day and to ensure that I'm healthy, fruitful, and successful, I have to get up early. I set my alarm for 5:00 or 5:30 a.m. each day. Funny thing about my body's first response to that alarm, though: "Hit the snooze!"

To stay healthy in my midsixties, I try to go to the gym five times a week. But, when I first wake up and remember the gym, my body says, "You deserve a break today!"

I frequently travel to speak and consult. When I'm in a large city, I love to stay at hotels that offer an omelet bar with a chef waiting to take my order. In one season I stayed at the same place in Chicago often enough for the chef to get to know me a little bit. When I walked up to order, he asked, "Pastor, do you want the usual?" (For me, the usual is an egg white omelet, spinach, no cheese, and whole-grain dry toast with a little bit of strawberry jam.) My body wanted to respond, "Heck no! I'd like that tall stack of banana pecan pancakes, and don't skimp on the syrup!" The body is a good servant, but it is a terrible leader.

I used to be a night person, always staying up late to watch Arsenio Hall (if you are old enough to remember who Arsenio is). But then I began to notice that Jesus had the discipline of being a morning person, no matter how demanding his schedule was. For example, in Luke 4 we read that Jesus made a house call to heal Peter's mother-in-law. (A quick side note: as soon as the mother-in-law was healed, she hopped out of bed and started serving others. Amen, sister!) Luke continues,

> At sunset, the people brought to Jesus all who had
> various kinds of sickness, and laying his hands on
> each one, he healed them. Moreover, demons came out
> of many people, shouting, "You are the Son of God!"

*But he rebuked them and would not allow them to
speak, because they knew he was the Messiah.*

(Luke 4:40-41)

In other words, on that occasion Jesus served others late into the night. Then verse 42 tells us, "At daybreak, Jesus went out to a solitary place."

I learned that I'd better get to bed earlier at night if I have hopes of being like Jesus. I won't miss my early-morning routine of daily devotion and prayer. When I do, it's too easy for me to stop being healthy and revert to being a jerk. So I practice this morning time with God each day, ensuring that my spirit directs my body and not the other way around.

At the risk of offending the night owls among us, I'll point out that research indicates morning people tend to be healthier and happier, and they accomplish more.[4] Of course, there are always exceptions. Many nights, my friend Adam Hamilton, lead pastor of The United Methodist Church of the Resurrection, the largest United Methodist Church in the country, doesn't even start his many writing projects until after midnight, and he is very productive. But, that's not the case for many of us. I know that once 10:30 p.m. rolls around, regardless of tempting distractions, I need to be in bed to ensure I maintain whole life health.

Seventeen years ago, I never darkened the door frame of a gym. I also ate what I wanted and when I wanted it. I was forty-nine years old, and that lifestyle seemed to be working for me just fine. I would pause long enough to think about getting a gym membership, and my body would say, "Nah, you might get hurt at the gym." I was happy to agree with my body.

Then, out of the blue, I collapsed onto my wife's lap in the middle of dinner at a Cincinnati restaurant. I had suffered a heart scare, and let me tell you, that was quite a wake-up call. I started to consider what was at stake if I didn't make my health a priority. My daughter had just graduated from college, and my son was just starting. They have since married great Jesus-following spouses and provided Carolyn and me with six incredible grandkids! Oh, what I could have missed out on if I had not learned to master my body and make it "get up" and do something that it had never done before.

The Word says, "Do you not know that your bodies are temples of the Holy Spirit, who is in you, whom you have received from God? You are not your own" (1 Corinthians 6:19). What is at stake in your life? What is God directing you to do—to be up on Sunday mornings in time for worship, improve your health habits, do daily devotions, find community in a small group?

The first step toward miracles of health and healing is to "get up."

PICK UP

After we get up, the second thing we need to do to activate healing in our lives is to *pick up*. Jesus told the man at the Pool of Bethesda to pick up his mat. Now, the man's mind had to be telling him it was impossible; he had been an invalid for thirty-eight years. But, sure enough, the invalid bent over and picked up his mat, able to do so through the transforming word of Jesus Christ.

God's Word is powerful. As the psalmist said,

> *Then they cried to the LORD in their trouble,*
>   *and he saved them from their distress.*
> *He sent out his word and healed them;*
>   *he rescued them from the grave.*
>   *(Psalm 107:19-20)*

You and I also need to "pick up" the Word of God. We need to exchange our limited thinking for the limitless thinking of Jesus

Christ. Our mind is to reflect the mind of Christ; that's the start of healing miracles.

The apostle Paul wrote, "Be made new in the attitude of your minds." (Ephesians 4:23). Later in that same letter, Paul referred to the Word of God as "the sword of the Spirit" (6:17). The Word is not to serve as our defense against the world but as our offense for enabling us to cut through any resistance that comes between us and God's miracles.

God has designed us to have power over our bodies. If my body registers thirst, I can tell my body to drink a glass of water. We also have power over our emotions. When I retain anger, it becomes a health issue. The stress of sustained anger builds up the level of cortisol in the bloodstream, which has numerous negative affects on our health. Our heart rate and arterial tension increase. Paul's advice applies here: "Do not let the sun go down while you are still angry, and do not give the devil a foothold" (Ephesians 4:26-27).

Controlling our anger has practical physical, as well as spiritual, implications for our lives. Impatience, frustration, fear, and the inability to forgive—a major issue for many people I've counseled—have much the same effect. We hold on to hurts and anger for decades and then wonder why our health begins to break down.

Positive emotions, on the other hand, help to foster health, as does exercise. We need to embrace the power of mind over body and its significance toward many of the miracles we are seeking. This power of mind over body is why Jesus often said after healings, "Your faith has healed you" (Matthew 9:22) or "Your faith has made you well" (Luke 17:19). Likewise, the apostle Paul confirmed a close tie between faith and healing. Paul was speaking to a crowd in Lystra when he spotted a lame man listening intently to his words. "Paul looked directly at him, saw that he had faith to be healed and called out, 'Stand up on your feet!' At that, the man jumped up and began to walk" (Acts 14:9-10).

Let's look at a few examples in the field of athletics. Spud Webb, a point guard who played basketball for the Atlanta Hawks, was five feet six inches tall. Yet Spud won the NBA slam dunk contest back in 1986 despite being one of the shortest players in NBA history. Just as amazing, he beat the defending champion, Dominique Wilkins, who was six feet eight inches.

In 1954, Roger Bannister was the first human being observed and recorded as running under a four-minute mile, a feat believed to be impossible by the medical community of the day. Bannister's record lasted just forty-six days, until another runner broke it. Now, elite high school athletes run sub-four-minute miles, reflecting the legacy of Roger Bannister, who understood the power of mind over body.

Our beliefs about God and ourselves play vital roles in our wellness. It's essential for our whole-life healing that, through picking up the Word of God, we replace our "stinking thinking" with the mind of Jesus. We are to remind ourselves daily that we are "fearfully and wonderfully made" (Psalm 139:14), that God desires for us to experience life abundantly (John 10:10), that "I can do all things through him who strengthens me" (Philippians 4:13 NRSV), and that God wants us to prosper through the work of our hands.

We have to guard ourselves against negative influences and negative self-programming as well. What are you reading? What are you watching? Who or what are you allowing to feed into your life?

One increasingly significant negative influence is pornography. As a longtime pastor, I have seen its devastating effects far too frequently. Pornography corrupts our view of what true intimacy can be within a marriage, and divorce rates for the past forty years have in part reflected that influence.

Another negative influence is toxic religion, mentioned previously, in which our view of God has been corrupted. The behavior of the "church folk" around us unfortunately can perpetuate rather than eliminate false perceptions about God. We even find hints of this behavior in the story of our healed invalid in John 5. When this man showed up at the temple, walking on his own two feet after an amazing thirty-eight years of being confined to a mat, the religious authorities did not rejoice with him. First they chastised him for carrying his mat on the Sabbath, and then immediately they turned their attention to the "law-breaking" Jesus, who had the temerity to heal on the Sabbath.

We need to grasp that God loves us and does not condemn us. Too much of what masquerades as religion is about "can't" and condemnation versus grace, healing, and hope. We will never open ourselves up to experience a deep inner work of healing and transformation until we trust that God does not condemn us. That does not mean that God expects us to stay where we are. As Jesus told the adulterous woman who had barely escaped stoning, "Go now and leave your life of sin" (John 8:11).

And so the former invalid, healed beside the Pool of Bethesda, had his whole life and life picture of himself turned upside down. His picture had changed from "I will always be this way" or even "I deserve to be this way" to being a new creation in Christ. As Paul wrote, "Therefore, if anyone is in Christ, the new creation has come: The old has gone, the new is here!" (2 Corinthians 5:17).

All healing is possible with God, and all of us benefit. The man at the pool picked up his mat and moved out into the community, positioned to become a source of new life, hope, and love.

WALK

After we get up and pick up, the third healing directive that Jesus gives is to walk. In other words, it's time to put the mind of Christ into action.

I frequently sit in denominational meetings, and the topic almost inevitably turns at some point to the shrinking size and decreasing effectiveness of the mainline church in the United States. Here is what is wrong: people come to our churches, hear the Word of God on Sunday, and then go away proverbially "living like hell" on Monday through Saturday. These may all be great, well-meaning folks, but the resurrected Christ has almost no relationship with their day-to-day experience. Some of us read the Word of God, know the Word, and possibly even share the Word, but we do not practice the Word. We don't activate the power of the Word in our lives. Paul tells us, "Whatever you have learned or received or heard from me, or seen in me—put it into practice. And the God of peace will be with you" (Philippians 4:9). It's time for us to put the Word into practice; it's time to walk.

My daughter Kristen is a pediatric dietitian, and my son Jonathan is an orthopedic surgeon. Both regularly see the devastating health consequences of poor diets and lack of exercise. Jonathan recently told me that he occasionally has to complete amputations resulting from uncontrolled diabetes while patients remain awake, because the patients' hearts were too weak to undergo general anesthesia; local anesthesia was safer. The Center for Science in the Public Interest has reported, "Unhealthy diet contributes to approximately 678,000 deaths each year in the United States, due to nutrition- and obesity-related diseases, such as heart disease, cancer, and type 2 diabetes." The center also indicates that obesity rates have "doubled in adults tripled in children, and quadrupled in adolescents" during the last thirty years.[5] Change for the better in our health habits is urgently needed.

At the same time, we can't be in a race toward health or life change. That's why Jesus' directive was to walk, not run. Walking means developing a pace that we can sustain for the long haul. It's more of a marathon and less of a sprint. The solution isn't a flash-in-the-pan effort or an easily neglected, too ambitious New Year's resolution. We must bring our bodies into submission and be transformed into the mind of Christ.

SPIRIT AND SOUL

Let's return to the invalid man at the Pool of Bethesda, because the most important point about healing miracles is yet to be made. In John 5 we read, "Later Jesus found him at the temple and said to him, 'See, you are well again. Stop sinning or something worse may happen to you'" (v. 14). Something worse? What did Jesus mean? I think it's clear that Jesus was referring to the man's soul.

God's number-one priority for healing miracles in your life is healing your soul. The soul is the center of your senses, desires, affections, and appetites. The soul, sometimes confused with the spirit, is in fact different. Soul and spirit are closely related but are not synonymous.

Our spirit is the part of us that either chooses or refuses to be connected with God. We read in Paul's first letter to the Corinthians,

> *What we have received is not the spirit of the world, but*
> *the Spirit who is from God, so that we may understand*
> *what God has freely given us.... The person without*
> *the Spirit does not accept the things that come from*

the Spirit of God but considers them foolishness, and
cannot understand them because they are discerned
only through the Spirit.

(1 Corinthians 2:12, 14)

When we are alive in the Spirit, we understand what God is calling us to do, yet we may become frustrated because we still can't bring ourselves to actually do it. The problem is that our souls still carry the residue of bad habits and poor life choices. We tell ourselves, "I don't have any self-discipline. I tried, but I just can't do it." We become convinced that we lack the power in our lives to overcome. Not true. Let's "pick up" the Word again: "For the Spirit God gave us does not make us timid, but gives us power, love and self-discipline" (2 Timothy 1:7).

We already possess everything we need through God's Spirit. We do not have to let anything defeat us, because we have been given the power to overcome. The problem is that we allow our bodies to take the lead and cling to negative thoughts instead of being renewed by transforming our minds in Christ Jesus. It's time to get up, making our bodies do what they do not want to do; to pick up God's transforming Word; and to keep walking, a long persevering obedience in the same direction.

YOU'RE NOT IN THIS ALONE

The story of the healed invalid in John 5 provides a great example of how miracles require divine intervention and our own human initiative. However, I want to be clear that pursuing healing is not just a solitary endeavor between you and Jesus; all of us need people surrounding us to provide coaching, support, counseling, and prayer, for both physical and spiritual healing.

131

Is anyone among you sick? Let them call the elders of
the church to pray over them and anoint them with
oil in the name of the Lord. And the prayer offered in
faith will make the sick person well; the Lord will raise
them up. If they have sinned, they will be forgiven.
Therefore confess your sins to each other and pray for
each other so that you may be healed. The prayer of a
righteous person is powerful and effective.

(James 5:14-16)

Community plays a crucial role in healing. A paralyzed man healed in Luke 5:18-20 only reached Jesus because four of his friends carried him on his mat to the home where Jesus was staying and lowered him carefully through the roof down to Jesus' feet. (I hope the homeowner had insurance!) After calling Lazarus out of the tomb, Jesus directed the community surrounding Lazarus to remove the grave clothes, freeing Lazarus from the final trappings of death (John 11:44). In case after case, Jesus' efforts were bolstered by friends and community interceding to foster miracles of healing.

HEALING IS ONLY THE BEGINNING

Miracles of healing and life transformation should be only the start of the story, not the end. Scripture gives several excellent examples of how the rest of the story should play out.

In Luke 4, Peter's mother-in-law did not stay in bed after she was healed; she immediately returned to serving Jesus and the guests in her home. In Luke 18, Jesus healed a blind man sitting by the roadside, and "immediately he received his sight and followed Jesus, praising God." That is, instead of the man throwing a party to celebrate, he followed Jesus and the disciples into the mission field and the evangelism business.

One of the most fascinating examples in Scripture is the healed demoniac in Luke 8. Jesus encountered the man when he and the disciples took a boat to a region known as Gerasenes. The healing by itself would have been extraordinary: Jesus ordered the demons to leave the man, and they entered a herd of pigs, which then rushed down to the lake to drown. What followed the healing, however, may have been even more remarkable: Once free of the demons, the man asked to follow Jesus. Jesus denied his request, knowing the healed man had a more crucial purpose. Soon, the former demoniac was an on-fire evangelist! "So the man went away and told all over town how much Jesus had done for him" (v. 39).

Even though Jesus seemed reluctant many times to have news of the healing miracles widely shared, time and time again those healed could not contain themselves, and they spread the news far and wide. It soon became a bit of an impediment to Jesus' ministry, because he would find afflicted people waiting for more of the same from him when he arrived at his next destination.

In Jesus' short earthly ministry, this type of healing was not his main focus. Even so, look at how powerful it was! We are always seeking to connect people with Christ. Sharing our stories of his transformational and healing work within our own lives helps to make that happen. Do not keep the good news of your miracle to yourself!

BIGGER THAN US

Miracles are to be bigger than just us. We and our churches are also called to be empowering centers for healing and renewal in our communities and beyond. We often hear the question, Why does God allow bad things to happen? Those "bad things" may include children starving to death in South Sudan, a coroner's office overflowing with overdose cases, refugees who have lost home and hearth, or racial tensions that erupt into violence in the streets. Sadly, the list goes on. First, let's set the record straight. God does not let bad things happen; we do. As we are healed, we are also to be healers, restoring the places long devastated.

Jesus' miracles were driven by his compassion. When he looked at the blind, the disabled, the hungry, the least, and the lost, he said, "I have compassion for these people" (Matthew 15:32). In fact, the word *compassion* comes up in the Gospels again and again.

> *When he saw the crowds, he had compassion on them,*
> *because they were harassed and helpless, like sheep*
> *without a shepherd.*
>
> *(Matthew 9:36)*

> *When Jesus landed and saw a large crowd, he had*
> *compassion on them and healed their sick.*
>
> *(Matthew 14:14)*

> *Jesus had compassion on them and touched their eyes.*
> *Immediately they received their sight and followed him.*
>
> *(Matthew 20:34)*

> *When Jesus landed and saw a large crowd, he had*
> *compassion on them, because they were like sheep*
> *without a shepherd.*
>
> *(Mark 6:34)*

It was Jesus' compassion for us that carried him all the way to the cross:

> *"He himself bore our sins" in his body on the cross, so*
> *that we might die to sins and live for righteousness; "by*
> *his wounds you have been healed."*
>
> *(1 Peter 2:24)*

Jesus bore our sins; it's already done. The least we can do is gratefully accept Jesus' healing for ourselves, and then, since we are Jesus' hands, feet, and bank accounts in the world, extend that compassion and healing on to others.

What is God calling you and your faith community to do? In what ways can you get up, pick up your mat, and walk on behalf of the world God loves? Where can you be agents of compassion, creating healing and hope?

Here is the good news: transformative miracles for healing are possible in your life and the lives of those you love. When we, as God's partners in mission, add our human initiative to divine intervention, we are positioned and called to bring about miracles of healing and hope for God's people. After all, "God's compassions never fail. They are new every morning" (Lamentations 3:22-23).

If you are struggling today in any area of your life, don't continue to live in defeat. Your past does not define you, nor does past failure control your future. God redeems. God restores. In Jesus, we are empowered to overcome any obstacle that opposes God's purpose for our lives, as we live out our days in health and wholeness.

REFLECTION

In your journey with Jesus, how will you activate miracles of health and healing in your life and the lives of those around you?

- Name an unhealthy habit you need to break. Find an accountability partner. Become part of a life group that will provide encouragement and accountability as you pursue life change.

- Take the first step toward physical health through exercise. Commit to taking the stairs, and fast from using elevators, escalators, and people movers. When you arrive for work or shopping, park in the space farthest from the door. At work, convert your sit-down meetings to walking meetings.

- Do you believe you could be struggling with chemical or alcohol dependence? Check with your physician about available treatments and treatment centers, and find a church-based recovery program for accountability and spiritual support.

- What is the most important new spiritual, emotional, mental, or physical practice for which you need to get up, pick up, and walk to achieve health? Commit to a plan of action, and take the first step.

- How can you be part of bringing health and healing to your community? We become healthier when we invest in helping others become healthier.

EPILOGUE:
RESURRECTION

Early on the first day of the week, while it was still dark,
Mary Magdalene went to the tomb and saw that the
stone had been removed from the entrance.

(John 20:1)

When you take a moment to think about it, it's funny how we choose to celebrate Easter, even in our churches. As a kid, dressing for Easter was a big deal. My sister and mom always wore pretty pastel dresses or suits with decorated Easter hats. Plus, no ensemble was considered complete without the requisite white gloves. My mother would deck me out as well. Even today at Ginghamsburg, where a guy wearing a suit to worship typically means he must be a first-time guest, folks tend to dress up more than usual for Easter Sunday worship. However, the first Easter wasn't exactly pastel eggs, fuzzy bunnies, and an Easter bonnet with all the frills upon it.

As Pastor Nadia Bolz Weber has said of Easter, "Really it's a story about flesh and dirt and bodies and confusion, and it's the way God never seems to adhere to our expectations of what a proper God would do."[1] As I was rereading the John 20 scriptural account of the resurrection this past spring, for the first time the words "while it was still dark" in the first verse caught my eye. Those words refer to more than just the sun not yet having physically appeared above the horizon; they describe the emotional, spiritual, and relational darkness that gripped Jesus' followers in that moment, a feeling of hopelessness and discouragement. Mary Magdalene had hurried to Jesus' tomb facing the sad task of preparing Jesus' body, and Jesus' closest friends were closeted away, fearful of arrest and persecution. Many of us today may find ourselves feeling more mournful than joyful, more fearful than optimistic. The headlines remain grim; some of our families—even entire communities— are struggling. Resurrection seems more like a pipe dream than a new-each-year reality.

When Mary found the stone rolled away and the tomb empty, she didn't conclude that Jesus had risen. Instead, with fear and grief, she ran to the disciples to proclaim that Jesus' body had been taken. Peter and John rushed back to the cave to confirm that it was true. Later Mary returned to the tomb, still grief-stricken and worried, and it was at that point that the risen Jesus, unrecognized by Mary, approached her.

Jesus asked, "Woman, why are you crying?" (John 20:15a). He was addressing Mary's personal state of darkness, even though by that time the sun could have moved up into the sky. In truth, Mary had arrived at the tomb early that morning expecting to find a dead body. In fact, the power of her expectation was so strong that she could not recognize the reality of the risen Christ now standing directly in front of her! Our expectations become the ceiling of our life reality.

This power of the mind, this power of expectation, is nothing short of amazing. Whenever I have to give blood, I am prone to passing out. I have what doctors call a vasovagal episode. When I think about the blood that is about to be drawn, the vagus nerve becomes stimulated, my heart rate and blood pressure drop, and there I go. It's all through the power of my expectation.

So, what expectations do you have right now that are holding you back and preventing you from experiencing the miracle of resurrection—a dying marriage, a dead-end job, a lost child, a missed opportunity?

Mary's expectation caused her at first to miss Jesus in the perceived darkness surrounding her. What is your perceived darkness causing you to miss?

Humans have an innate fear of darkness. When a few of my grandchildren spent the night with us recently, I went upstairs to kiss little Luke good night. He hugged me tightly and urgently reminded me to leave the door open just like Mommy had left it. Luke wasn't taking any chances with monsters under his bed. Such fear isn't unique to children. You may have monsters of your own. What if I get in a wreck? What if I can't get that promotion? What if our marriage doesn't work out?

Darkness is unavoidable. All of us are going to experience dark times. But the fear of possible or imagined dangers lurking in the dark can hold us back from experiencing the miraculous that is possible all around us.

How easily we forget that we are never alone. Jesus has been right in front of us all along, and God has appeared in the darkness since Old Testament times. When the Israelites spent forty years in the wilderness after escaping Egypt, God led them in a pillar of cloud by day (Exodus 13:21). Later, "the people remained at a distance, while Moses approached the thick darkness where God was" (Exodus 20:21).

For nearly twenty years, Carolyn and I lived in the darkness of a struggling marriage. It was only after we changed our expectations and dropped the word *divorce* from our vocabulary that our marriage was able to find miraculous resurrection. We have now been married forty-six years. Do you feel dead in your marriage? Is your job not working out? Check your expectations. David proclaimed in Psalm 62:5, "My soul, wait thou only upon God; for my expectation is from him" (KJV).

Remember that your "next" can be better than your "first."

> *The* LORD *will make you the head, not the tail. If you pay attention to the commands of the* LORD *your God that I give you this day and carefully follow them, you will always be at the top, never at the bottom.*
>
> *(Deuteronomy 28:13)*

Resurrection expectations will activate your breakthroughs!

Jesus, having asked Mary why she was crying, then asked her a second question: "Who is it you are looking for?" (John 20:15b).

It was the right question. Sometimes, like Mary, we forget that God's miracles are the *who*, not the *what*. We think if only we could get the what—the right job, the right relationship, the right amount of money—then everything would be fine. But it's an illusion. As Augustine wrote in his classic *Confessions*, "Thou hast made us for thyself, and our heart is restless until it finds its rest in thee."[2] Who are you looking for? Sometimes we fail to see Jesus because of our faulty perception of who the risen Jesus is.

In the garden, Mary thought Jesus was a gardener. He must have little resembled the picture of a white, angelic-looking Jesus that some of us admired on the wall of our Sunday school rooms while growing up.

So, how do we find and recognize the risen Christ today? We can find the answer in the Gospel of Matthew:

> *"'Lord, when did we see you hungry and feed you, or thirsty and give you something to drink? When did we see you a stranger and invite you in, or needing clothes and clothe you? When did we see you sick or in prison and go to visit you?'*
>
> *"The King will reply, 'Truly I tell you, whatever you did for one of the least of these brothers and sisters of mine, you did for me.'"*
>
> *(Matthew 25:37-40)*

To experience the miracle of resurrection each day, we can't simply look to the historical Jesus or the Christ of the printed page; we must recognize and be in dynamic contact with the living Christ of today. Author and business executive Juan Carlos Ortiz writes, "A knowledge of the historical Jesus is static, so it doesn't generate growth. But to know the present-day Lord, that is dynamic. You know Him, and you go on knowing Him all the more. You know him better today than yesterday."[3] God is not concerned about making you religious; God is concerned about making you new—resurrected to a new way of thinking, to a new way of being, and to new expectations.

Mary finally understood that she was in the presence of the risen Christ when he called her by name.

Jesus said to her, "Mary."

She turned toward him and cried out in Aramaic, "Rabboni!" (which means "Teacher").

(John 20:16)

Today Jesus is calling you by name, inviting you to step into your own miracle, beckoning you to risk forward in faith into God's miracles, for the good of the world that God so loves. Today is the day of salvation! Throw off everything that hinders you, and let's invite God to transform our ordinary into God's extraordinary. Then, together, we will change the world one life at a time—starting with our own.

Notes

Chapter 1

1. Loretta Ross-Gotta, *Letters from the Holy Ground* (New York: Sheed & Ward, 2000), 17.
2. Cardinal John Henry Newman, "God's Will the End of Life," in *Our Faith and Belief: A Carefully Selected Compilation from Great Writers...* (New York: Murphy & McCarthy, 1917), 33.
3. David Van Biema, "Mother Teresa's Crisis of Faith," *Time,* August 23, 2007, http://content.time.com/time/magazine/article/0,9171,1655720-1,00.html.

Chapter 2

1. Eric Metaxas, "Bonhoeffer Never Said That!" (blog), June 10, 2014, http://ericmetaxas.com/blog/bonhoeffer-never-said/.
2. Frank Raj, "Gandhi Glimpsed Christ, Rejecting Christianity as a False Religion," *Washington Times,* Dec. 31, 2014, http://www.washingtontimes.com/news/2014/dec/31/gandhi-glimpsed-christ-rejecting-christianity-fals/.
3. Erin El Issa, "2016 American Household Credit Card Debt Study" *Nerd Wallet*, December 14, 2016, https://www.nerdwallet.com/blog/average-credit-card-debt-household/.

Chapter 3

1. Jonathan Marlowe, pastor of Chapel Hill UMC and Midway UMC in Reidsville, NC, included this quotation in his blog, which was taken from a sermon he wrote about ten years ago on Trinity Sunday. The blog is no longer available. (E-mail message, August 22, 2017.)
2. Kathy Gannon, "A Woman Sacrificed for Honor of Her Family," *Los Angeles Times*, July 9, 2000, http://articles.latimes.com/2000/jul/09/news/mn-50070.
3. Neal Wooten, "Making God in Your Own Image," *Huffington Post*, January 23, 2014, http://www.huffingtonpost.com/neal-wooten/making-god-in-your-own-im_b_4066571.html.
4. Mark Berman and Samantha Schmidt, "He Yelled 'Get Out of My Country,' Witnesses Say, and Then Shot 2 Men from India, Killing One," *Washington Post*, February 24, 2017, https://www.washingtonpost.com/news/morning-mix/wp/2017/02/24/get-out-of-my-country-kansan-reportedly-yelled-before-shooting-2-men-from-india-killing-one/?utm_term=.30b43197b246.
5. Jason Hanna, Kaylee Hartung, Devon M. Sayers, and Steve Almasy, "Virginia governor to white nationalists: 'Go home...shame on you,'" CNN, August 13, 2017, http://www.cnn.com/2017/08/12/us/charlottesville-white-nationalists-rally/index.html
6. Will Willimon, *Fear of The Other* (Nashville: Abingdon Press, 2016), 16.

CHAPTER 4

1. Aly Weisman, "14 People Who Failed Before Becoming Famous," *Business Insider*, February 20, 2014, http://www.businessinsider.com/people-who-failed-before-becoming-famous-2014-2?op=1/#yonc-lost-on-star-search-in-1993-1.
2. Kelly Dwyer, "Was Michael Jordan Really Cut from His High School Team," Yahoo Sports, January 10, 2012, https://sports.yahoo.com/blogs/nba-ball-dont-lie/michael-jordan-really-cut-high-school-team-215707476.html.
3. Oswald Chambers, August 2 entry, *My Utmost for His Highest,* New International Version (Uhrichsville, Ohio: Barbour Publishing, 1992), 157.

CHAPTER 5

1. Richard Rohr, "The Gate of Heaven Is Everywhere: Breathing Yahweh," *Richard Rohr's Daily Meditation,* October 6, 2014, http://myemail.constantcontact.com/Richard-Rohr-s-Meditation--Breathing-Yahweh.html?soid=1103098668616&aid=W6_U3gyEM9g.
2. Marie Barnett, "Breathe," on the album "This is the Air I Breathe," © Copyright - Pacific Arts Group / Pacific Arts Group.
3. Ann Voskamp, *One Thousand Gifts* (Grand Rapids: Zondervan, 2011) 58.

CHAPTER 6

1. "Leading Causes of Death," National Center for Health Statistics, March 17, 2017, https://www.cdc.gov/nchs/fastats/leading-causes-of-death.htm.
2 "Overweight & Obesity Statistics," National Institute of Diabetes and Digestive and Kidney Diseases Health Information Center, October 2012, https://www.niddk.nih.gov/health-information/health-statistics/overweight-obesity.
3. "Amid Opioid Overdoses, Ohio Coroner's Office Runs Out of Room for Bodies," KIMIKO de FREYTAS-TAMURA; *New York Times*; February 2, 2017, https://www.nytimes.com/2017/02/02/us/ohio-overdose-deaths-coroners-office.html?_r=1.
4. Lauren Gelman, "8 Surprising Health Advantages You Have as a Morning Person," *Reader's Digest,* accessed May 31, 2017; http://www.rd.com/health/wellness/morning-person-advantages/.
5. "Why Good Nutrition is Important," Center for Science in the Public Interest, accessed May 31, 2017, https://cspinet.org/eating-healthy/why-good-nutrition-important.

EPILOGUE

1. Nadia Bolz-Weber, *Pastrix: The Cranky, Beautiful Faith of a Sinner & Saint* (Nashville: Jericho Books, 2014), 173.
2. Dan Graves, "Our Hearts are Restless," Christian History Institute, accessed May 31, 2017, https://www.christianhistoryinstitute.org/incontext/article/augustine/.
3. Juan Carlos Ortiz, *Living with Jesus Today* (Carol Stream, IL: Creation House, 1982), 73.